It's a Dick Thing!

Secret Thoughts of Silent Men

Compiled and Edited by Don Koberg

Writer's Showcase

San Jose New York Lincoln Shanghai

It's a Dick Thing!
Secret Thoughts of Silent Men

All Rights Reserved © 2002 by Donald J. Koberg

Writer's Showcase
an imprint of iUniverse, Inc.

For information address:
iUniverse, Inc.
5220 S. 16th St., Suite 200
Lincoln, NE 68512
www.iuniverse.com

ISBN: 0-595-22780-5

Printed in the United States of America

To silent men everywhere who might be encouraged to speak.

CONTENTS

Preface ix

Man-ifesto xi

Prologue xiii

Editor's Note xvii

Part One: Ever a Boy 1

    Snakes and Snails and Puppy Dog Tails *George McKamy* 2

    Mountain Men Have Feelings Too *Robert Amon* 5

    E. Clampus Vitus Treks to Colma *Kent Bittleston* 6

    Late For Dinner *Mike McGee* 10

    Forgive Us Our Trespasses *Alex Gough* 13

    Gotta Go *Don Dennison* 19

Part Two: I Am Man. Hear Me Weep! 27

    A Deeper Cry Within *Bob Banner* 27

    Tears *Archie McLaren* 36

    Running With Jack *Jim Bagnall* 39

    Magic & Loss *John Thomas* 43

Part Three: Me and Them 46

    In Passing *Gil Cooke* 46

    Porky *Milt Mannix* 48

    Sing In Me Muse, And Through Me Tell The Story *Steven Foster* 51

    Another Goodbye *Josef Kasperovich* 54

Centerfold

    Jehovah Gives Witness *Roberto Armstrong* 56

Part Four: It's a Dick Thing! 75

    Heat of the Moment *Dana Jones* 75

    "Mr. T" *William Stansfield* 80

Fruitcakes *Don Koberg* 83

Revision *Steven deLuque* 85

Me *Steve Omega* 87

Whatever *Robert O'Brien* 88

Part Five: Secrets **89**

Truth Telling Is the Best Aphrodisiac *Bob Banner*..........................89

The Wake *Douglas "Doc" Moxness* 92

Perspective *Ron Thompson* 98

Confession *Craig Nuttycombe* 100

To Be (a Man) or Not To Be. Is this a Question?

   Christof Hillebrand..101

Part Six: Fatherhood **104**

Hiding Out *Barry Williams* 105

Fathers *Bill Kiely* 110

After Shave *Stacey Warde* 114

Additional Poetry

Bob Banner *Feeling the Feelings?* 24

Ray Clark Dickson *When the Well Blows*....................................18

                Viagracias 80

Patrick Germany *Happy Birthday To Father* 104

Don Koberg *Boy Toy* 9

                Self-Inflicted 113

Tom Law *Cycles* 12

Milton Mannix *Papa* 110

Jack Random *All Around You* 34

PREFACE

There's More to Men than Masculinity

Thinking people no longer need science to convince them that a complete human being, whether physically classed as male or female, is actually a bit of both. Yet, with the women's liberation movement cresting after nearly fifty years of struggle and the men's backlash movement on the rise, any discussion regarding sex or gender requires clear eyes and an open mind. Like walking a tightrope, it requires a balance of knowledge, skill, and sensitivity. As for politics or religion to reveal one's views on this most delicate of subjects evokes immediate and varied deep-seated reactions. Sadly, the issue is further complicated by the fact that traditional social mores, religious tenets, and governmental rules persist in defining the separateness rather than integration of genders.

The result has been that when today's males express their manliness in its total human dimension in the face of the one-sided demands made on them, all manner of both cheers and boos ring out. In the past, the odds against achieving equilibrium have deterred the majority of males from even trying to express their wholeness. Those brave enough to experiment have tended to over-compensate and usually learn the hard way that too much or not enough of either masculine or feminine behavior leads to sure-fire failure in both sectors.

In the process of collecting the material for this book, dozens of real and ordinary males were asked to contribute a short piece expressing some aspect of their maleness. Initially, nearly all, in spite of being non-writers, were instantly intrigued with the opportunity to speak from within the protective company of brothers. Later, after weighing the potential criticism their words might provoke, the majority reneged. What follows is what remained; a sampling of work by the bravest of predominantly silent men.

Every man is a volume if you care enough to read him.

MAN-IFESTO

We are warriors and we are peacemakers. We do battle and we repair. We are the sentries, armed and battle-ready, guarding the gates. We are the corpsmen, vulnerable and caring, nursing the wounded behind the walls. We are the butchers, bakers, bankers, and ballet dancers of a wide-ranging gender. We are male, sons of parents from Mars and Venus, products of the balanced species called Human.

As in all species, our strengths and weaknesses evolve naturally. The precept that men must dominate is lore and not a natural given. We assume the responsibility of leadership as a function of being husbands and fathers protecting our families and homes. Ever responding to cues from natural selection, we proceed to fulfill our destiny while seeking to improve body and mind.

We may vary between 'bad ass' and 'candy ass' and all that lies between. Whether we choose to represent ourselves as silent, senseless, brutes or as verbal, wise, and brave defenders of truth, or some combination of both, our worth and credence can only be fairly judged in terms of how well or poorly we play our stated role.

We are tolerant, sharing, supportive mates and parents whose true freedom and strength comes from within. Whatever our aims, whether to function as driving rivers of mighty power or as gentle waves smoothing the shore, we singularly and collectively contribute to the process of becoming a vibrant whole.

PROLOGUE

THE MAN WAS BORN FOR TROUBLE
(Homer, The Odyssey, (IV, 350)

Steven Foster; Outreach program mentor

The word, "Odysseus," is from the Greek odyssesthai—"to hate," or "to be angry." Autolycus is said to have translated the name as "a victim of enmity."

No doubt it has always been in the nature of a man to be angry, to feel victimized, to contest his fate with gods and men. He is just as quick to consider his own karma his enemy as he is to seize it as opportunity. The labyrinth he must negotiate in order to reach home all too often seems unreasonable, hopeless, unjust. He blames the gods almost as much as he blames himself. But to publicly acknowledge his own complicity in what has come to pass is to admit his own weakness and stupidity. Caught in the Catch 22 ("whose fault is it?"), he erupts in helpless anger.

He well knew what he was getting into when he landed on the island of the Cyclops. From a distance he had watched that "brute so huge, he seemed no man at all" walking around like an earthquake. He'd even had a premonition that "Some towering brute would be upon us soon." It was his idea to take his best men and venture into the giant's lair and pilfer whatever wasn't fastened down. He paid the price: "No pretty sight, it turned out, for my friends." Two by two the monster cannibalized them, until only six remained.

If the gods don't bring it on, we bring it on ourselves. No matter how loudly we lament our fate, the truth remains. "The man was born for trouble." Leave your beautiful wife alone at home for 20 years and you've got trouble. Fall asleep at the tiller and you've got trouble. Kill the cattle of the sun god and you've got trouble. Eat of the lotus and you've got trouble. Blind the eye of Cyclops and you've got trouble. Mock the god of the ocean winds and you've got trouble. Keep your arrows in your quiver, and you've got trouble. Pull them out, and you've got trouble. Keep your manhood hidden, and you've got trouble. Pull it out and make love, and you've got trouble. Steer to the right, steer to the left, and you've got trouble. Do nothing, and you've got trouble. Keep thinking how to win the game, and you've got trouble.

Who among us would be foolish enough to boast that we were free of trouble? We were all born for it. We make trouble with whatever we do; we find it wherever we go. Is it any wonder that we should be so angry, that we should want so badly to get home? But rage brings us no closer to our goal. Rage only twists us into ragged strangers begging at the back door. If we express our anger, if we lament our woes, we only attract more strangers. Trouble goes where trouble is. And, if we hold our anger in, letting it build within us, the caldera cracks open and we spew forth frustration like a pestilence. We murder; we make war; we raid cities; we lay waste; we contend with one another; we hurt the ones we love most; and we consume ourselves and each other with guilt.

When the time comes, and it always does, for us to go into the cave where the blinded Polyphêmos roars like thunder, there are but two options. One is to be eaten alive by trouble. The other is to trick trouble into letting us go for a while. I'm in favor of the second alternative. And I am now convinced that the only way to get free is to admit, like Odysseus, that I am nothing. To say, "My name is Nobody: mother, father, and friends, everyone, calls me Nobody." So trouble, please leave me alone for a while. I am, after all, not the least bit important.

Nobody is everybody. Not Bill, or Pete, or Odysseus, but any man who was born for trouble. Not the great so-and-so, but the usual asshole, the stupid, vain-glorious, egotistical, generic asshole, like you or me. If we can cultivate this anonymous assholeness within ourselves, this acceptance of our karma, we may stand a chance in this life, and elude the fate of our brothers who were eaten alive.

EDITOR'S NOTE

The challenge to compile an anthology of men's writings developed after reading several collections by women celebrating their multi-faceted womanhood. Outspoken and unabashed, the female wisdom and wiliness projected in those works were clearly intended to serve as guidelines for less verbal women. I liked most of what I read.

What troubled me was their overtones of feminist dominance and the generalized portrayal of men as insensitive, non-verbal, and brutish creatures, attributes attainable by both sexes yet definitive of neither.

I thought it unfair. My friends and I weren't anything like that, except of course when we chose to be. In the main we were trustworthy mates and lovers, hardworking providers, and capable fathers. Such debasing of males as mindless, angry, doltish, beasts of burden, best left to their own senseless pleasures, needing only to be fed, petted and prodded, as one might train animals, demanded correction.

One specific collection of female memoirs that finally triggered me to action included a memoir written by my own daughter describing how much fun it was to be part of a group of girlfriends with similar interests, including dressing as poodles to appear at pub events and store openings.

I'd been a proud Poodle Papa from the start having painted their stage curtain, taped their performance, applauded their success, and taken pride in having a published author in the family.

My initial reaction was "What's the big deal? Guys have always done things equal to that, just not so cute."

To set the record straight, I determined to expose and thereby clarify the naturally wide spectrum of real male behaviors, from the gentlest and most caring of men to raging militant chest beaters. From that moment to this, my task has been to create a forum for the truly multi-layered male to state his case in print and while encouraging other men to speak out, let readers determine the truth.

In the process of egging cautious non-verbal men to face issues of gender and come to terms with their views in print, I quickly passed through the looking glass of introspection into an arena of unsuspected activity.

My conclusion: Yes, 'lone wolves' do occasionally gather to interact, 'strong and silent' men do weep aloud, and 'angry bullies' still flail and rave. Within these pages a range of humble voices, from contra tenor to basso profundo, combine to form the choir celebrating the reality of true manhood.

There will always be a battle between the sexes because men and women want different things. Men want women and women want men. **George Burns**

Part One:

Ever a Boy

Enjoying "a boy's night out" is a common manly desire; for some it's an absolute need. Although taking a deserved break at the lodge hall or neighborhood tavern away from the demands of routine is no longer gender specific, it seems that men will never cease reverting to boyhood behaviors when freed from adult responsibility.

In this section, six manly individuals, community contributors all, each one little different from the guy next door, across the street, or down the block, describe their separate versions of escaping, however briefly, from the expectations of society.

Snakes and Snails and Puppy Dog Tails

George McKamy, University Staff Engineer

I remember
When little boys were made of "snakes and snails, and puppy
dog tails",
And men grew within the rhyme.
But, little boys are made of cool wintergreen,
Fresh, sweet nectar and a tad bit of thyme.

I remember
Little boys grew to become men
In a world upside down,
Where little boys and men played with rules
That turned their life around.

I remember
The heart and soul of little boys and men misunderstood
In expectations and forgotten dreams
That passed between their schemes.

I remember
When a world of little boys and men's joys
Being hero or not,
Where the differences were in the toys they got.

The missing rationale from folk lore that boys are made from "snakes and snails and puppy dog tails" and "girls are made of sugar and spice and everything nice" has always been a mystery to me. Why must boys be bitter and ugly when girls are so sweet and loving? It has always seemed that, despite sexual preferences, men differ little from women. Both boys and girls learn from life and parents and take those instinctual and learned tools, the basics for survival, along their chosen paths to adulthood.

My parents followed the rules of tradition and passed them on to me. Mother taught me "social" survival skills in lessons of nurturing and love, in caring for others and to forgive, ("Love thy neighbor as thyself"), even the importance of domestic responsibilities in cooking, sewing and cleaning, all practical means of survival.

Father taught me the guts and glory of never backing down from a fight, never to start one, but never to run, to stand tall and be a man in the midst of adversity, (remembering all the while that "men don't cry" and "boys are not supposed to hug and kiss boys"). He taught me practical lessons of work, how to mow a lawn, rake leaves, build fences, slit a lamb's throat, butcher a pig; pluck feathers from a chicken and break down a side of beef; but he could never get me to love football, or boxing.

Together, my parents taught me the importance of love, of family and friends and of God and church and self. I learned to stand proud of whom I am, to cherish personal honor and loyalties, and be a leader. They taught me to trust, to respect my elders, to protect those less fortunate, to be a gentle man and say 'Please' and 'Thank you' when asking a favor. "Please pass the potatoes". "Thank you". When leaving the dinner table I was taught to ask permission before leaving. When moving between others I was told to say: "Excuse me please".

Kneeling, each and every night, humbly repeating the prayer, "Now I lay me down to sleep. I pray the Lord my soul to keep. If I should die before I wake, I pray the Lord my soul to take…God bless Mommy and Daddy and Sister and Brother", I learned from my parents a prayer to God. Meal time prayers gave thanks for the food "we are about to eat" and for the protection of each and everyone one of us, family and friends and strangers alike.

I was taught to not honk when picking up a date, to open the door for her; and to walk on the "outside", so to better protect her; and never to strike a woman.

Somewhere along the way, I lost balance in the "appropriateness" of such behavior, because I was also taught that boys could only show affection to girls. The result was that before my teens, I wished many times I were a girl. They were able to show affection by hugging and kissing little boys, and other little girls; plus they could cry.

My parents have taught me well in traditions handed from one generation to another; and with the best tools they had to offer. I have no regrets. I may dwell in misunderstanding, or lack of knowledge, but without regret.

Much of my training remains with me in practice to this day. What saddens is the realization that I now live in a world callously indifferent to my education, where all that I learned seems impractical, even lost as we enter the 21st Century.

Somehow, the rules have changed mid-game. I don't think girls care if I honk when picking them up, or if I open the door for them, or on which side I walk. Foul language and violence seem ordinary, a mere difference of opinion. Religion has taken newer forms. Trust is a belief. And, as for boys and girls, it is still said that boys are made from "snakes and snails and puppy dog tails" while girls are "sugar and spice and everything nice".

I'll be damned if I know why.

Icebergs

Writers of both sexes often generalize men as akin to icebergs with but a fraction of their chill selves revealed. Anyone truly interested need only look beneath their surface to find brave hearts, tearful warriors, and bawdy vaudevillians, all anxiously vying for attention and love against heavy social odds.

Mountain Men Have Feelings Too

Robert Amon, Retired Broker

The Oxford Bar in Missoula, Montana never closes. It does, however, manage to comply with State law by not selling any alcohol between 4:00 and 6:00 AM. The remaining patrons, of which usually there are many, simply mosey down the bar to the food-service counter and kill the two-hour hiatus breakfasting on the house specialty: cow brains and eggs. Then they repair to the back alley and puke their guts out. To Mountain Men, this is considered to be a "feeling", as in, "I feel like I'm gonna puke my guts out." Other guy-feelings in the Rocky Mountain West include the following:

She:	"Good morning, honey, How ya feeling today?"
He:	"Hung over, babe."
She:	"So, lover, what do you feel like doing this weekend?"
He:	"Nuthin', babe."
She:	"Hey, sweetie-pie. D'ya feel like taking some line-dancing lessons?"
He:	"I feel like I'm gonna puke my guts out."

In addition to "gut-feelings", Mountain Men also must live with something known as the "Continental Divide". This is a little-understood line on the map that wanders through the West for no apparent reason. One theory is that men born on the East Side of the line feel they must become cowboys or loggers, while those from the West Side tend to move to Los Angeles and become unemployed movie actors or Scientologists...or both.

So far I have alluded to four typical Mountain-Man emotions:

1. Stomach-ache
2. Headache
3. Laziness
4. Fear of dancing

There may be other feelings too, I suppose. And perhaps these (and the others) are common to men everywhere. Maybe, even, to a few chicks. But that's just too much to ponder.

E. Clampus Vitus Treks to Colma

Kent Bittleston, Electrician

Some guys might generalize to think of me as some sort of 'frat boy' or 'lodge member' but I'm not. I'm a Clamper, a member of E. Clampus Vitus, San Luis Obispo Chapter 1.5, which, although brotherly in practice, is separate from those norms and far more than either of them.

An outgrowth of an ancient fraternal organization, ECV was revived in California by hard-drinking, fun-loving sourdough miners during the gold rush heyday. It soon became dedicated to the preservation of historical sites, events, and persons which otherwise might be overlooked or forgotten.

Being historically oriented and hysterically practiced, we generally have a hell of a good time in the process. In fact the prime requisites for becoming a Clamper, besides an interest in the history of the West, are a sense of humor and a cast-iron stomach.

We don't have meetings. We have gatherings called "doin's" where absurdity and tomfoolery govern and copious quantities of alcoholic beverages are consumed. One of the largest gatherings, my favorite, is an annual trek to the peninsula town of Colma to celebrate Emperor Norton's Birthday, which takes place in January. Joining a caravan of men always seems a good way to start the New Year.

Joshua Norton, Norton I, Emperor of the United States and Protector of Mexico, exemplifies the ECV motto: "If it's absurd, I believe it." Norton, self-ordained benevolent despot and legendary lunatic, a failed Forty-Niner entrepreneur and eventual beggar/ benefactor, became saint to some and madman to others.

For quite a few years now several of us "boy-men" have made the weekend trek. On Friday, our cars and trucks are packed with an assortment of sleeping bags, guitars, duffel bags, beer coolers, black hats, black coats, black vests (the ECV translation of traditional sourdough garb) and Red shirts (honoring their red wool long johns). With radios blaring, we head north. It doesn't take long for the coolers to open and joke-telling to start.

An hour later and hungry, we stop for dinner at Lugarcito, the best Mexican café in King City where man-sized bowls of tortilla chips and salsa, and platters of ceviche, Camerones Diablo, Pescado Frito, Pulpo, Chile Verde, all washed down by bottles of Modelo Cervesa Negro fill the bill.

Stuffed, we're back on Highway 101 for more music and jokes about the cute senorita waitress. Nothing serious is ever allowed. In another hour, on Rocks Road close to San Juan Bautista, we stop again where a huge lady, always happy to see us pull into her parking lot, runs a vintage smoke-filled tavern with a good selection of tequila. While bringing our hostess up to date on Clamper nonsense, we stretch our legs and belt down a few jiggers. Then, making sure the sheriff is nowhere in view, we continue north with more music and a story or two about hefty women; never serious.

Our goal for the day is a modern condo with guest bedrooms and baths, TVs, and DVD players in the Silicon Valley. It's nice enough but nothing like the old ranch house in the hills of Saratoga, once our first night's haven where, with more drinks and endless talk, we dozed off watching porno films via Super 8 and slept on the floor, couch, extra bed, or anywhere that space allowed. We still drink and talk ourselves to sleep in the condo, but the ambiance sure has changed. We now watch Chicken Run.

Waking up Saturday morning to the smell of fresh-brewed coffee is a manly prelude for our final leg to Colma. We dress in Clamper best and head for Batech Brothers Liquors, our regular pre-celebration stop-off for pre-ordered pork tamales. Those tamales are so damn good. Standing around in a Cupertino parking lot at eight thirty in the morning drinking bag-wrapped Tecate cervezas and gorging on fresh tamales is clearly one of the reasons that memories of Norton the First remain in our hearts.

Colma Cemetery is packed with Clampers when we arrive. The Yerba Buena Chapter Band provides an off-tune background for speeches, dedications, hand-shaking, more beer, and the repeated phrase, "See you at Malloy's."

Each January Malloy's Bar, a Colma, California landmark and E. Clampus Vitus mecca, honors the Emperor with an annual crab feed. Organized as a fund-raiser by several Clamper Chapters, members travel from Washington, Oregon, Nevada, Arizona, Utah, and all parts of California for the event. Buckets of cracked crab, The Clamper Band, old friends, and generally high spirits prevail.

It's a man's day. Although the few ladies in attendance are extremely popular, it's here where we can become borrachónes, smoke black cigars, talk rough, lie about sexual adventures, and never worry about being corrected or judged. Last year, a woman sitting at the bar made a point of wanting to dance with the trumpet player. To catch his attention, she cuddled up to him and did a little shimmy. I watched as he fittingly pushed her away. "Get back Lady. I'm playing here," he said. His band plays together but rarely and there was no time for physical females.

Hours later, as the party winds down, we head back to the sterile condo in the valley for a final parking lot barbecue, some wine, a recap of the day's events, and eventual sleep.

Sunday starts slowly. After too much fun and too little rest, thoughts of driving back to San Luis Obispo add to the lethargy. We pay our tab, make plans for next year, and point the car southward, back to normalcy.

Boy Toy

Don Koberg

Momma loves me yes I know
For her nipples tell me so.
Hugging me tightly
Her tongue tickles my navel
Blowing fluttering raspberries
Evoking girlish giggles
I am the baby doll boy.
Why do I pull away so repulsed
Yet so intrigued?

Forget me now and join the crowd
Hang in, hang right and tight
Join the team, fight for God, play to win
Bring home the bacon
Flex your balls
Become a man
But don't forsake me
O my darling baby doll.

> **What's in a Word?**
> (Webster-wise)
>
> Dick: A Man or Fellow
> (Chiefly British)
> Dick: A Detective
> (U.S. slang)
> Dick: A Penis
> (Vulgar; slang)
> Dick: The name Richard
> (Generic Form; familiar)
> Dickens: Satan; the Devil
> (Early form of Dick)

Late For Dinner

Mike McGee, Water Resource Consultant

I was late for dinner the other night. I'd stopped by my shop and got sidetracked. Three guys who share the space with me were hanging around. While we talked I had a couple of beers.

There was Joe, quietly smoking a joint and drinking a Diet Pepsi. Joe's a big guy with laborers hands (He'd put you in mind of Lenny in Of Mice and Men). When I asked him "how's it goin'?," I got back "I lost another one today". Seems Joe feels the need to talk to terminally ill folks, says "dying is a lonely thing, and if I can be a friend for a while it sure makes the transition easier."

And, there was Sammy who spent his 21st birthday in Folsom Prison. He'd been there since he was 18. Went to jail for cutting the throat of his sister's boyfriend when the bastard beat her up. Fortunately he didn't kill the guy or he'd be there today. Sammy felt he had to join the Aryan Brotherhood just to save his butt, both figuratively and literally. He's about the best appliance repairman in town, owns his own shop, even though he had to petition the State for a business license. Sam will help people that can't afford to fix or buy stoves and refrigerators by just giving them an old one he's fixed. Having basically become a man in the joint he still has a lot of demons chasing him and regularly tries to kill himself.

The third fellow was Gary, the erstwhile leader of the pack. The toughest member, who can never seem to quite get over being known as "Cactus" and can't ever quite get his shit together, mostly because he's always trying to get other people's shit together for them, for instance, talking Sammy out of suicide at least three times or providing Joe a quiet place for dealing with mortality. Gary can barely read or write but is one of the best carpenters I've ever seen. He can eyeball a roof hip joint, stair risers, or grades better than most can with levels, calculators and transits. Problem is getting him to the job able to work.

Then there's me, Mr. Underachiever, who never lives up to his potential, the guy who everyone used to say was "so smart." "You're much smarter than your sister, why can't you be more like her?" (Me in a dress at Mardi Gras doesn't count here). I've worn out more careers than most guys have shoes. Never could figure out what to be when I grew up and still don't know if I ever will.

So, a couple of beers later I go home. I'm feeling pretty good but on arriving I'm berated for hanging out with my "low-life friends." As I'm having a very nice dinner with my beautiful, hard-working, and attentive wife in our fine home with all our wonderful possessions around us, I'm feeling guilty about once again disappointing her. I start to think to myself, who's really the low-life in this scenario?

Maybe a large part of this "dick thing" has to do with self-esteem. Males seem to either have too much, or not enough. We're always looking for it and either can't find it or can't recognize it when we see it.

CYCLES

Tom Law, Neuroscientist; poet

You can just barely see them —
high, inkspots against a cloud
clear at the top of the hill
shadows flowing down the oil-dark stream
hell-bent in black, coming this way.
Black flies with silver eyes
on the back of a tar-black snake
twisting hip dance
snake dance
slither down
the mountain
dance
one speck
rises
flies
over
the high side
down
the long slide
rider on the sky
one down
don't stop
roll on
bottom out
Flat dust ribbon writhing on sod,
aimed this way, viper whispers a guttural snarl,
dragonhead parting the wind, spitting flies.

Here they come, knees locked to iron-cold power
humping on the rib-throbbing wind's embrace
hurtling past on whirling galaxies
twin doughnuts spun on comet rims
glittering spokes stretched to the torus' edge
elbows resting on the planet's curve
dome light a star's reach above
figureheads planing on the gale's wake
white bone of air whistling in their teeth

Slip their grip on the grill of wind
and all idle down in the grinding gravel;
kick out the left third leg,
lean the brute to rest;
breathe out the slippery tension of the slowing world
and the universe lies still:
ticking,
cooling down.

Forgive Us Our Trespasses

Alex Gough, Realtor, Regional Historian

Dissolve to fifty years ago. I was already in hot water at Mission High School. We had a new principal, Sister Stephanie. That summer, between my sophomore and junior years, I had rolled my car on the Cuesta Grade that winds down from the mountains into town. There were four of us and we'd been drinking beer all night. I was 15.

We were hitting maybe 105 in my '49 Ford when we reached that last tight curve at the bottom. A rear tire blew and we went into a long elliptical spin, round and round. The back end of the car crashed into a raw cut in the mountain and we rolled over.

Except for Dallas, knocked out cold, none of us were scratched. We crawled out, pulled Dallas out of harm's way, and started running through the sagebrush towards town. When we finally reached the Cadillac dealership at the end of Monterey Street, good old upperclassman Ralph Franzone, out early on his paper route, picked us up and drove us home. Next day, the police came to the door. I had a lot of explaining to do.

Well, OK, word gets around, and maybe Sister Stephanie did have a little cause for concern. But I really did clean up my act once school started. I got elected Class President and went to work on the yearbook. There was one little problem. I didn't get along with J.D. Phillips, the basketball coach and former star at Cal Poly. I had bad-mouthed him to the point that he tossed me off the team. It wasn't that he didn't deserve it. At any rate, I got assigned to a PE class with the rest of the rejects. Understand that back then at Mission High, if you were male and hale, you usually played all three major sports. That year our football team won the conference and all but three or four boys in the entire school were on the league winning team. So PE, as opposed to the sport in season was definitely the bottom of the barrel. Anyway, one day we losers showed up for class and the coach didn't. I don't remember his name, but he was probably some Cal Poly PE major making a few extra bucks. While waiting, we decided to shoot some hoops on the outdoor asphalt courts but first, we needed some equipment, specifically a basketball. The balls were stored in a locked shed, the door made of scrap lumber. Somebody—I don't think it was me—said "Let's force it open", and someone else—not me for sure—did it. We got the balls, that was that. Then the coach finally shows up and turns us in for breaking the door. Before you know it, we're all sitting in Sister Stephanie's office, sweating it out. "We're going to sit here until one of you says you did it". And for a while we did.

Ephraim Escobedo, was one of the group. Now Ephraim was very quiet and had always been deferential to anything resembling authority, which in those days came in black and white, and nun was the number. So Ephraim says, "Sister, you mean you're going to make us sit here until someone says he broke that door?" "That's right, Ephraim!" "OK, Sister, then I did it". "Ephraim," she said, "I don't believe you, but you are all dismissed." Ephraim became my best pal after that.

That night, despite the fact that it was Thursday, the next day a school day, Ephraim and I had planned on going to a dance in Pismo Beach at the Rose Garden Ballroom. Harry James, believe it or not, was playing and an event like that couldn't be passed up. Guys like us would go to a dance and never dance a dance. We'd just hang around smoking cigarettes and maybe slip out now and then to have a beer in the car. But as luck would have it there was to be no money left over for beer that night. Before we left town, Ephraim's folks got a phone call from Sister "S". They barely spoke English but she got her message across that their son would have to pay for the door—$15—a lot of money in 1952. She said the nuns were worried about Ephraim, and wanted him to stop by the convent that evening.

On the way to the dance, we stopped at the nuns' house. Ephraim went in and I waited in the car, maybe half an hour for him. When he came out, he was crying. "What happened", I asked. He said they had really lit into him, telling him he was going to hell if he didn't change his ways and in any event he would have to pay for the door before he did. They even asked him if he had ever used marijuana. Now we really didn't know what that was. We had only vaguely heard of it, but it did sound like something we might want to look into. They also got it out of him that we were headed for Pismo instead of staying home to study.

An hour later, we were at the Rose Garden, on the sidelines as usual, scoping chicks, being cool, smoking cigarettes. Well, who should walk in but Assistant Pastor Father O'Sullivan. The minute I spotted him, I knew that Sister Stephanie had put him on our trail. "What are you boys doing here?" he asked. Now you need to know that although I had no problem bucking the lines of a coach like J.D. Phillips, I had always done an end run around real authorities like priests. We tended to treat them, even the more benign ones, like rattlesnakes—we gave them a wide berth. Father Daly, the pastor, had put the fear of God and priests in all of us. When he passed out report cards every month, heaven help you if you hadn't done well or spoke out of turn or displeased him in any way. Public humiliation was the least of his punishments. The worst might be getting slammed against the blackboard. He was a real prick. Ordering his minions to hose the swallows nests off the eaves of the Mission proved it. He evidently drank a lot of the sacramental wine and had a big red Jimmy Durante-nose to show for it. Behind his back, we whispered "inkadinkadink-inkadinkadoo."

So here comes Father O'Sullivan, looking down his red nose at Ephraim and me with his question, and I answer. "What am I doing here, Father? I might ask you the same thing!" Too surprised to answer, he merely spins on one heel and exits. I'm feeling pretty good with myself for being so brave.

Later, when we leave, there he is waiting for us in the parking lot wedged between a couple of Pismo Beach cops.

"Ephraim", I say, "Let's have a little fun." So we beat them to my car, a cool little '36 coupe I talked my mother into buying for me to replace my wrecked Ford, jump inside and try to look suspicious, like we're smoking marijuana or drinking booze under age. Sure enough, here come the three inspectors. Seeing nothing incriminating inside the car, they search the trunk. I can't stop from goading them on. "Don't touch that tool box." Of course they rip it open, only to discover...tools! Innocent on all accounts, we were freed to go and that was pretty much it for the night except for laughing all the way home.

Next day at school, I'm about five minute late, which means I miss roll call. I arrive just as class begins. "Where were you when roll was called", the nun asked. "I was here, Sister" "I don't think so" said she. "You'd better go see Sister Stephanie and get a tardy slip". So I did, and blithely too, never considering what was waiting for me. In her office Sister "S" was gripping the desk so tightly it seemed like her fingernails would pierce through the top, her neck rigid as a rack of over-wrought guitar strings. "Good morning, Sister", I optimistically say. "I need a tardy slip". "No one found in a Pismo dive on a school night get's a tardy slip. YOU'RE EXPELLED!" she blurts. And that was my last day at Mission High, the cheerful little school in the shadow of the concrete "M on San Luis Mountain, one day to be reborn as Mission College Prep, home of the Sisters of the Immaculate Heart of Mary.

Flash forward to tonight and the movie "Himalayan" playing at the Palm Theater. In the story, the elder about to die makes peace with the young chief that he has to that point bitterly opposed. He speaks in a whisper, but for me the words ring out loudly.

"A real chief must first disobey."

Trumpets sound, the Red Sea parts. I see the truth behind Icarus flying to the sun, Einstein flunking math, Henry Miller railing against his censors, John Brown raiding the armory, and the South rising up again and again. From Dada to hip hop, it's that moment in time when some cool underdog looks his 'massa' squarely in the eye, smiles, and spits out an ineffable retort, "Yassa". "Render unto Caesar what is Caesar's" and no one quite knows what to do with you. It's why we love James Dean and James Brown and why Paco de Lucia takes his mother's name as his own and why a punk singer names himself Marilyn Manson or Jello Biafra. The man the Greeks would have us know as Jesus—Yohoshua his real name, his mother not Mary but Merriam, the meaning of which is rebellion—the son of man is the son of rebellion, the depth of his rebellion cloaked in the mystery of the obvious. If that sucker won't shut his trap, kick him out of the Garden.

It ain't always pretty, but face it guys, underneath it all, the most important part of us flies below radar. And sure, there's mo' to the sto', and if you want to get technical you can find the schematic for the other half of the equation in Dumbrowski's great Hegelian book, "Creative Disintegration." And yes, there have to be skinners as well as hunters, catalogers as well as creators. There you have it. That's the story of the glory in a nutshell —the touch-stone of manhood.

I disobey, therefore, I am man.

When the Well Blows
Ray Clark Dickson, Poet

The smell of sweet crude
swells the air like Texas ticks; roustabouts,
shouting, laughing, roll in the slick,
eager for cash bonuses, Saturday night baths,
soaping down in hot copper tubs in town;
celebrate life in the long liquid
darkness, each star becoming mother, father,
sister, brother–
even the fancy woman who rocks him in her
blue-collar crib
knows his thoughts as he looks out
her curtained window at tall derrick shadows
dancing like scarecrows
in cornless fields.

Humankind when living is soft and tender;
When dead, they are hard and tough.
The ten thousand creatures
And all plants and trees
While they live are supple and soft.
But when they die: hard and stiff.
So it is said: what is hard and stiff
Belongs to death;
The soft and tender belong to life.
Therefore, the weapon that is too rigid
Will shatter;
The tree made of hardest wood
Will break.

Tao Te Ching

Gotta Go

Don Dennison, School Administrator

Brothers, have you gone through the annual "leaving with the guys" catechism yet? You know the dialog: "Do you have to go?" "Yeah, I gotta go." You stand there thinking, "I hope that does it" and start to move on, But no. "Well why can't we go too instead of just you and those guys?" Then you know you're in for it. That's when things start falling apart. Perhaps you're feeling mentally nimble and pass the buck. "The guys are counting on me." Or, head down and shuffling your feet, you spout something truly lame like "I don't know" or, in the spirit of true male collaborative communication, you say nothing, shrug your shoulders, and walk away. Well, listen my brothers in arms. I am going to give you the definitive answer to the age-old feminine road block question: "Why do you have to go?" Use it as you see fit. It's a bit long (which, based on the male theory that if a little works, more is better, makes it good). You may want to use only excerpts in preparing arguments of your own design. Just make sure you get yourself out the door when you 'gotta go'. Everyone, including the women, will be better off for it in the long run.

You sit there saying to yourself, "Ok, but that's not enough to really get me out the door." To burst free of the gravitational pull of home and hearth you have to have the rest of the story. It all goes back to a 1960's TV series called "Stoney Burke".

At thirteen years old, I was at home in the family's TV Room, nursing a King Size Coke every Tuesday night all by myself. It was good being alone without distractions from my favorite show. Stoney was a rodeo cowboy "bronc" rider and he had four friends that were his best buddies. In every show some big problem affected one or more of these five guys and they all covered each other's back, stood together and worked it out. For me, the best moment of each episode, the part I could count on every time, was the ending. With the stirring "Stoney Burke" theme music playing and credits rolling, Stoney and his four pals walk from the corral, their arms on each others shoulders, smiling, laughing, glad to be friends and together and satisfied that they were able to fix things up. It didn't make any difference how many times I saw that scene. I'd sit there grinning at the TV thinking to myself, "That's what I want. To be part of a group of guys who would do anything for you and you would do anything for them, guys I could always count on to come through for me in thick or thin, guys who'd be my best friends." I'm not sure the series had the same affect on every Holden Caulfield that saw it. However, "Stoney Burke" created an early awareness in me that began a lifetime search for fulfillment. The longing I'm talking about is the undeniable male need to be strongly connected to at least a few male friends and to have opportunities to hang together in some mutual endeavor. And in my case, that means at least once every year my male friends and me 'gotta go' back-packing in the mountains. In the world of men I'm not alone. Other men must feel the same urge and they all can't have watched "Stoney Burke."

But if you're looking for someone to blame, blame Stoney Burke. That's where it started for me. At least that's where I was first consciously aware of wanting that kind of camaraderie. It took me quite awhile to find it. Growing up, I wasn't very athletic but I assume that most guys resolve their male bonding needs with team sports. When I did start playing sports they were individual sports, one on one, not a team working together. I started back-packing with the YMCA when I was in high school. Despite publicity claims to the contrary, the "Y" did not exactly provide the bonding advertised in flyers. I was in graduate school before I began hiking with the same two to four guys year after year. It was then that I finally realized that I found what I had been looking for. We'd reach the summit of a pass together, after helping each other all the way, then look for half an hour to find a perfect camp site to cook and talk for hours at the end of an exhausting day, and in the morning, down the trail back to the trailhead at the end of the trip. We were Stoney Burke and friends walking together across the corral. We had done something. We had counted on each other. We had watched each other's back and we had seen it through to the end.

What about the counter argument, "Why not take your wife along or better yet, the family?" My response is, "When the chips were down, Stoney counted on the guys." I have backpacked with women individually and in groups. And I've gone with my family. Although each of those experiences was unique and enjoyable to varying degrees, none were anything like going with the guys. I'm not saying it is only women who have trouble appreciating this. Even other guys make comments like, "How do you fit your drums in those packs?" Or they ask about feathers and face paint or get weird about that Burt Reynolds movie, "Deliverance". O.K., until you've experienced it yourself that programmed reaction is understandable. Aside from my annual family negotiation, I feel no need to justify this to anyone.

It is not about guys going off together and being gross. It is not about telling dirty jokes or belching and farting by the fire. It is not about babe stories or checking out women on the way to and from the mountains. Although I would certainly be lying if I said that stuff doesn't happen. But it is not about that. It is not about "Iron John"-type men's encounter groups. We share the load. We help each other out. We leave each other alone. We laugh a lot. We've been known to cry. Over the course of five to seven days together our conversations run the gamut of sports, politics, the economy, jobs, kids, friends, experiences, memories, dreams. We talk, but it is not just about conversation. One thing we don't talk much about is our wives. There seems to be some kind of unspoken law there that would be too close to breaking a trust. We know our wives worry periodically about these conversations but we really don't go down that road. Maybe that assurance alone is enough to open the front gate.

It is doing something difficult together, encountering obstacles and working together to overcome them. It's a knowing that if the other guy needs you or you need him, a hand is there. It's about not always having to feel responsible or to be in charge. And it's about sharing: sharing water, sharing the job like gathering wood, sharing an orange, sharing a comment on the beauty surrounding you, sharing a story, sharing a thought.

I can't begin to tell you or even honestly remember the thousands of soul healing, personally enlightening, side-splitting funny, dumb and dumber, humanly touching moments that have occurred on these trips. They are unique and essential to my well being. They make me appreciate what I have left behind and those to whom I come home. They consistently make me a better person. I feel these moments are impossible to find and experience to this degree in any other setting.

Every trip has a finale; coming back down the trail together, repacking the car. We are tired, dirty and proud. We are leaner and better fit than when we started. We have been covering ground for the last few miles at a good clip, anxious now to get back, moving together in the rhythm that has developed after days and miles on the trail. We cover the last few yards. Gratefully take off our packs. Open the car. Get out the cooler hoping those beers we left on purpose stayed cold at high altitude. Pop that beer. Take a swig and look at each other and smile. I tell you it is Stoney Burke and his pals leaning against the corral and flipping a rope. At that moment, and in the memories that are savored over the months till the next trip, there isn't anything better. And that, brothers and sisters, is why I gotta go.

Freely admitting to your faults in no way frees you from seeking ways to correct them. (Fortune Cookie)

The husband who knows much more than his wife must surely know enough to keep it to himself. (Anon.)

Feeling the Feelings?

Bob Banner, Window washer; Publisher; Poet

I hate, I compete, I'm jealous,
I get angry, I want to fuck hard
I want to win
Fear rules my feelings
Expressing them is wrong, my head says
First from my parents
then from the counter-culture
Next from esoteric metaphysics
They are all telling me "No"
Keep it together
Don't say what you really think and feel
Keep your voice shut
They will hurt you if you speak up

Stay the soft male, the pretty one who
refuses to grow up
Maintain your indulgences with
seeking pleasure and distractions
Don't feel your pain, your anger, your violence
By expressing them you will be like them
By not expressing them you will have
transcended them and your example
will bring in a new age

Yes, stay asleep soft male
and more violence will leak out
from your denial
more haughty arrogance and self-righteous liberal piety will
ooze out and pollute your soul

Yes, stay soft and don't really feel
what you're feeling
don't grow up
Keep repeating the repressions

OR you can take a chance
and listen to your feelings
feel your feelings
feel the deep cry that sits in your
guts ready to wail away

Feel the ruthless anger awaiting
eagerly to express its natural rage
Feel your spirit waiting to emerge
from its hidden place
from its secret protective cell
waiting for purifying safety

Heed the wild man oh soft male
Get dirty, get messy
Get crazy
Roar with guffawing hearty laughter
Wail with tears streaming through your eyes
Rage with teeth and fists clenched to kill
Feel the ecstasy of a calm centered mind

Feel the mystery that is unfolding as you take back your life.

"Perhaps one of the most self-enhancing experiences a man can have is to observe two women making love. To observe the caressing and tenderness that creates fulfillment without a penis-hard or soft. The security that it offers him about the nonessentialness of his penis to sexual satisfaction can allow him to treat his penis as a nice addition rather than a prerequisite to his sexuality." Warren Farrell, Ph.D., WHY MEN ARE THE WAY THEY ARE, Berkley Books, 1988

PART TWO:

I AM MAN. HEAR ME WEEP!

If boys aren't supposed to cry, where is their proper alternative human outlet for reacting to loss, sense of helplessness, and the suffering of others?

The tearless man, for centuries trained to hang tough, stifle all expressions of pain or fear, an insensitive bulwark of manliness, finds that he is a misfit in today's more humanly integrated world. Trapped in a time warp of contrary expectations, he cautiously and somewhat apologetically, opens up.

Meet five regular guys who, typical of the majority of their brothers, do weep (however alone and unnoticed) for many of the same concerns affecting all humankind.

A Deeper Cry Within

Bob Banner, Window washer; Publisher; Poet

We need to cry. No question about it. But how nourishing is the simple act of crying? And what are the different levels of crying—from the single tear falling down one's face to the deep

27

wailing where one goes out of control and unashamedly lets loose one's deep grief? We may feel sad because of a certain song on the radio, or a scene while watching a movie—the situation triggers within us an urge to cry. Perhaps a few tears will ooze out. And then perhaps there will be a feeling of satisfaction or a freshness that often comes from crying. But is it nourishing? Does it genuinely go deep into our bodies and souls so that we feel fed, so that we feel bigger than we are, so we don't sink into self-pitying which most crying is.

Crying for the most part is obsessive self-pity—a bewailing of one's worries and difficulties—a simple release of tension which actually perpetuates the prevailing sadness or melancholy. It often does not go deep enough to actually move into other uncharted areas.

There's a deeper cry in us that aches to emerge, but is frustrated by mind and memories of possible pain that we prefer to keep hidden from view. Most men I know won't cry, let alone allow themselves to wail deeply. We were brought up to control any tear that began to well up in our eyes or hearts.

And even the simple need to cry superficially gets halted by fears of being labeled a sissy, weak, etc. But then on the other hand there are men who can easily cry yet their tears carry no potency, no power, no bigness in the cry, only an impotent spasm of release, remaining in the realm of ordinary sadness.

There is so much sadness in the world, no doubt about it; but it stays on a certain level that is mediocre, bland and relatively comfortable. Look at people's faces as you walk in any city. See the sadness, the depression, the fears, the melancholy—and look deeply at what's behind it. The pain of an abused/abandoned childhood, the abandonment of a lover, friend, parent, the not having anyone to share one's obvious secrets, doubts, seething anger that cannot be expressed, and on and on and on...

We may go back to our isolated apartments, lonely rooms in shared-housing whether with strangers or "family" and may shed a few tears in the privacy of our own pain. And sometimes, when we are moved beyond our mind, to cry because of an immediate crisis—a friend's surprising suicide, an abandoned lover, the death of a close relative—we still will often tolerate the privacy of our grief. We will close our eyes, put our faces into our hands and find the closest private room where we can be alone with our anguish.

Yet, some people have had moments when they surrendered to the anguish so much that they needed to share their grief with someone else. To share one's grief with open eyes and open arms where one is transported to a place beyond mind, beyond expected conservative ritual, beyond what others may think, is a most beautiful act. It's a gift from the heart.

It's a cry that comes forth from the belly that is messy, that brings forth mucus from the nose, tears that pour out, a cry from the throat that is connected to the belly and the heart (not cut off from one's guts). This deep cry, when uninhibitedly expressed, can move others—simply move others to also feel their own pain, whether it's despair, longing, suffering, ones difficulties or simply feeling the other with no mind, no triggers necessary.

And most often, when we surrender to this type of expression of grief, there will be a lightness, an expansion, an unfolding of Being that emerges. It feels safe to come out since the heart gives breath to its existence...

I've seen many people cry. From self-pitying spasms of a few tears to full-blown wails where the need emerged uncontrollably and full-out. And sometimes there are powerful feelings of grief, need and longing that have not been so expressly cathartic yet are felt right to the bone.

I remember a man who was so triggered by a woman's deep feelings of grief that he immediately went to a deep place of surrender and unashamed expression of his hurt. There he was all bundled up in a pile, a semi-fetal position where grief had overwhelmed him. When the facilitator asked, in a whisper, where he was, he simply muttered "in a dark room." The loneliness was inexhaustible, the pain seamless, the deep cry endless. The facilitator asked him what he wanted. Unashamedly, he answered "mommy." He continued saying the word until he was actually crying out for her. "Mommy, mommy, where are you?" She wasn't coming. His despair and grief and loneliness grew.

Suddenly, mother did show up and the man panicked. The facilitator asked what was happening. Mother had come and she was mean and cruel. A terribly vicious voice came from the man's voice, "Shut up—just shut up and quit your crying." Panic and terror and a heavy panting surrounded the man. Here, what he longed for, waited for, needed—did in fact come—but with it came terror, wrath, a viciousness that was unwarranted. The man, too vulnerable to return to grief and too scared to feel angry at the abuse, lay there stuck in panic, hysteria, panting, wanting to run away. Someone mildly suggested to him, "Hush!" Suddenly his breathing eased; the panic subsided. Slowly, very slowly, he began to reach again for what he needed. His arms formed a gesture of need—a simple need to be held, touched, to be loved. He reached out for her hands and arms and legs and moved closer to her, a gestation of simple need on his lips. Sensitively the facilitator placed her fingers in his mouth. He sucked. He was being fed, simply. No more grief, simply a man/child sucking hungrily on basic nurturance from a woman's finger-nipple. The aggrieved man/baby had become happy because very basic needs were being met. Cooing and googling sounds emerged naturally from his voice. Soon his slurping turned to giggles and a sense of relief circled the room. Laughter and lightness filled the air. Having surrendering deeper and deeper to his needs while soaking up the simple love absent in his childhood, he lay there satisfied for twenty minutes more.

When he finally returned to being the adult, his face had changed—lighter, brighter, happier, smiling with an ease, his eyes full of light and spirit. I spoke to him much later and asked how he felt afterwards. He said that for about three hours he had a sensation of being acutely and sensitively alive. His stomach had expanded and felt quite huge. No tension. His head felt very light as if "mind" had gone outside to play. He had felt a wise child-like state come over him and remain. And, because of this raw and naked sensation he was more sensitive to people, to their masks, their lies, their deceptions, their walls of protection. He told how he'd felt the need to be protected, to be placed like a seedling in a sanctuary-like place to grow in safety. Yet, he still felt responsible to stay and contributed to the group's activities. Later that night he wrote a poem. I believe it will clarify my story.

Twitching, squirming, rocking in agony,
trapped wounded animal seeking escape only to find
numbing as its route to consolation...
Wanting, needing, crying out for Mommy
Only to find when she arrives I am terrified
by her wrath and scorn and abject cruelty
Drama endlessly repeating itself
Past haunting present
Creating petrified personal history to pass along to
future generations

No one could take the pillow away from me
No one could take spirit away from me
They could pump me up with rules and regulations
and stomp my creativity and damage by body
and screw up my mind
But they couldn't take away spirit

Writhing in agony I reached out and found Anne's hand
I take it desperately
and begin sucking —
Breast of life and nourishment
So mad and wild in desperation to cling to another human, my
species
Panting hysterically
doubting safety and stability
Fearing my revealing, my undoing, my unfolding

Someone whispers to hush
The panting suddenly stops
Desperation eases away
Past mother of cruelty dissipates into now
New mother of Anne is now there
I can finally breath slowly and deeply
deeper and more relaxed than ever
Soaking her in
Soaking every cell of love
Letting it all go through the baby who now begins to
gurgle sounds of newly discovered memories
Moving to be held in her arms
still soaking in streams and streams of
energized loving—replenishing cells of
crystallized repression

Gates are torn asunder
Genuine fragile tenderness and soul nourishment
soothingly enters and fills me up
expands and softens my childlike belly
Suddenly gurgles turn to giggles
soft cooing of innocent laughter
Sated baby now smiling and giggling and googling in the present
Slowly I move to Cathy's legs and arms
resting my light head full of space and
expanded no-mind
Belly full yet very sensitive to
falseness and lower vibration in the room
terribly sensitive—too raw and naked to live here...
needing protection, sanctuary
for birthing this non-alien alien
the Real Self
with an inherent knowledge thirsting to be used
lying dormant waiting to peek out
and speaks its true voice and name...

I share this story to suggest the many levels of feelings that are trapped within us; that we need to be intimate with all of our feelings whether they be rage, grief, joy or ecstasy; that we need safe places to let ourselves go into feelings that are welcomed (not shunned and repressed) so that we can reclaim those feelings, reclaim hidden spirit so that we may live a more passionate, full-bodied life and once again move in the world like warriors, with both vitality and vulnerability, power and grace, potency and innocence.

All Around You

Jack Random, Poet, Pornographer

When I die
Fold me naked
Into the
Beautiful black flesh of the earth.

No coffin fortress
Against my mother,
No formaldehyde
Lip stitching denial
Of the
Soft Machinery of life.

Let the gentle sex
Of the probing root life
Trail downward
Along the white arches
Of my cathedral bones.

Let the holy orgy
Of the earth
Fill my domed skull
With the
Gentle loving of the world.
Each year
Fold me naked
Back into the warm flesh of my mother
And I will become the loving earth.
I will spread my spirit
On the wind.

I will have eyes of
Green roses.
I will have
Blood in the sea,
I will have
A consciousness of grass,
And I will have
Arms in all the green
Hills of the world.

Arms vast enough at last
To hold all my million children.
From my warm bed
I will be the sun's lover
And a
Magical brother to the moon.

I will trail
Sidelong and downstream
And I will be your food,
Alive in every
Apple fruit,
Awake in the falling
Arc of each cherry blossom.

Once dead
And in the earth,
Now immaculately dissolved,
I will be there when you
Burst the veiny flesh of a peach.
I will be all around you

And silently knowing,
This is my body
Bursting for you.
Take,
Eat.
Pass me
Hand to human hand
And lip to perfect lip.
Let my name dissolve
With my flesh
But when you
Drink the blood
And eat the smooth flesh of the earth,
I will be alive,
And awake,
And all around you.

Tears

Archie McLaren, Fund Raiser, wine consultant

I've always cried at movies, even as a pre-teenager in the early 1950s. I never considered such an emotion unnatural, although as a young man in the South a male only exhibited what were considered "manly" characteristics, and crying of any sort was most certainly not one of them. In fact, it was cooler to be cruel than to be sensitive; hence, the casual, unconscionable manner in which some young white men mistreated black people, throwing eggs at their houses and calling them vile and demeaning names. Upon reflection on those confusing and troubling times, crying for the sorry state of Caucasian awareness would have been quite appropriate.

Killing non-domesticated animals was also a sign of manhood back then. Many young men had BB guns, and the coolest of all had 22 caliber rifles or went with their fathers into the woods to shoot shotguns, sort of the ultimate macho goal of young teen-age hunters. Birds of any sort were fair game for BB guns in one's own neighborhood and back yard. I believe that boredom contributed to the carnage. When there is nothing to do, and there often wasn't, just shoot something! One day, I saw two sparrows on a rose bush in the back yard. I took aim with my BB gun, hitting one of them. The other did not move; it looked at me as if it could not believe what I had done. I walked directly to it, saw the dead companion on the ground, and as the remaining sparrow looked at me, I shot it as well. I returned to the house and cried for them and for my stunning cruelty and insensitivity and never picked up a gun again.

I cried three times in junior high and high school, once after changing schools in the eighth grade, when three boys standing in front of the school responded to my question about the location of the Principal's office by turning their backs on me. I didn't cry in front of them. I was insecure enough about my family's lack of money and about the way I had presented myself to those privileged young men. I waited until I got home and then relived the experience. In fact, I relived it over and over again. I can see their disdainful looks to this day, and can feel my hurt and anger at the time. It has diminished somewhat, but it has not gone away. I wish I could forget that sort of experience once I have assimilated its lessons or benefits; some things are unshakable.

The second time was when our junior high school team lost the county junior basketball championship by a single point. We had a terrific team, very capable of winning and we young men took athletics very seriously. I don't recall having seen anyone else cry. I was too absorbed to notice. I think I cried for all of us, because I felt that each person was experiencing his own level of frustration and disappointment. I suppose winning meant more to me. Athletics provided a ready excuse to leave the house and its parental inhabitants, and to release frustration in general. On the down side, there was the frustration of losing when something that you considered substantive was on the line. Now, in retrospect, I find it easy to celebrate the dance, as opposed to the battle, of athletics, especially when playing with someone who feels a similar harmony with that dance. It is a game after all, not a war or test of manhood. The third time was when my first girlfriend dumped me for a guy with a car, not just any car, a brand new 1957 Pontiac Bonneville Convertible, a veritable jukebox on wheels. I lost ten pounds in the process. My athletic achievements suffered, and my grades dropped. I was "pricked on the thorns of life," and I was bleeding. I cried, at least once in front of male peers who thought me very uncool, and my girlfriend's pals got a great laugh when the love letters I'd written to her were read aloud. I sang sad and romantic songs to myself, which I am certain helped only to exacerbate my self-indulgent angst.

Then I found another girlfriend, and things improved until I more or less followed her to college in 1960, where she dropped me within a week or so of our arrival, this time, not for a guy with a car, but for one who was significantly more accomplished and certainly more mature than me. I didn't cry that time, nor did I cry again for any reason for almost a decade. I wonder if my potential sensitivity for other circumstances and issues suffered because of my more self-contained approach to relationships and if I have ever truly allowed myself to love a woman since.

The most powerful and memorable experience, about which it is very difficult, in fact impossible, to recall without tears, is the death of Martin Luther King and the subsequent memorial march that took place in Memphis in1968. Another young male teacher and I had been traveling together in the South. We had taken his sports car, which had no radio, and entered Memphis unaware of the tragedy that had occurred. It was night and the city was virtually dark, with few lights on the roads or in houses and almost no cars on the streets. It was an eerie feeling, similar to what one might experience if everyone had suddenly died. We soon found out that Dr. King had been assassinated, and that a march was to be held in protest of his death and as an affirmation of his spirit. Organizers of the march wanted there to be silence; consequently, when the procession began not a word was spoken; the only sound heard was the shoes of what seemed to be one hundred thousand people hitting the pavement. Watching, I felt compelled to join in. I have never participated in anything so profoundly moving. What has been even more lasting, and increasingly difficult to tolerate, is the realization that someone, not unlike an unthinking boy shooting birds with a BB-gun, murdered that fine man. Fortunately for us all, his ideals are everlasting.

The people who influence how we shape our lives are those who love us most and those who refuse to love us **Anon.**

Running With Jack

Jim Bagnall, University Professor, Emeritus; photographer

Tuesday was bad. There was pain, bravery, and the desperate but futile attempt to comfort. There was no doubt about it. Tuesday was hard, but the image is soft, a blur of grief. There were tasks to be done, the kind that drain energy yet keep us connected. Tuesday was bad but Wednesday was worse, the start of a new life without Jack.

I wasn't prepared for Wednesday. It was on entering campus to teach my class that I encountered the first cruel hole his absence ripped from the fabric of my life. Missing would be the joy of meeting him there to share a discovery or to plan a mischief over coffee; those meaningful pleasures we both took so lightly were now cut short never to be continued as before. I feared that even the memory would begin to fade like a weathered storefront sign on a once vibrant business.

My studio class was a blessing that morning. I knew I wasn't really there for them. In spite of my distraction and lack of energy, twenty creatively active students helped the morning pass without tears.

At noon I had to get away. I went to the gym, changed into running clothes, and started out, heading toward the hills behind the campus. Running faster than ever before, I didn't know whether I was escaping my loss or in search of a better way to deal with it. Without destination, I kept going upward, always up. When paved streets turned to dirt roads, I kept the pace, my heart thumping. Unreleased sobs stuck in my throat.

Soon beyond the range of other runners, I was finally by myself, alone in the hills, and the tears were at last free to flow. It was then that I realized that I wasn't alone. Jack was still with me.

It had been ten years since we'd met. So many events during that time remained clear like those tracks left by seabirds on the beach below his ocean studio. I'd been hired to teach with Don, a former mentor, and moved south from Berkeley with wife, two sons, lock, stock, and barrel. A few days later, Don took me aside. He wanted me to meet a guy who knew more about more things than anyone he'd ever met and I was introduced to Jack. It was true. Jack was metallurgist, physicist, and chemist, father of eight, cook, philosopher, salesman, teacher, technician, artist, humorist, and socio-political critic. He'd been in the Navy, sailed around the world, feared neither man nor beast and owned a parrot, exotic chickens, and a goat. I'd grown up in various cities, held degrees in Psychology and Architecture and had never known the likes of Jack. He was indeed unique, the sort of person any man could learn from no matter how much they thought they knew.

Being accepted by Jack meant passing his test of genuineness. In the weeks that followed my preferences in all categories were evaluated for superficiality and, when differences of opinion emerged, were debated, at times late into the night over a full fifth of bourbon. Then, one night after a huge meal with our families, all fourteen of us, I said exactly the right thing to seal our friendship.

"I'm building a freeze-drier," I said.

Jack said, "Uh huh."

"I'm using an old vacuum cleaner and the tank from a water heater," I said.

"That won't work. What the hell are you going to do with it anyway," he said.

"I could freeze-dry pork chops for camping," thus inventing the absolutely correct response.

It so happened that Jack loved pork chops. He said, "Come on down to the studio tomorrow. Let's talk about those pork chops."

We never did devise a workable freeze-drier or do anything with pork chops except eat them, always charred over a fire of distressed wood and smelling and tasting of paint thinner and creosote. It was those pork chops that served as the connective thread woven throughout the fine linen of our 'unconditional' friendship. With Jack, there were no conditions involving friends. He gave freely to one and all but giving to friends, unconditional friends, was his greatest joy.

I remember his call late one night, middle of the week, a school week. He'd driven his old VW van to L.A. for supplies, broke down half way home, and was stuck in Goleta. There was no doubt in his mind that I'd drive the three hundred miles round trip and tow him home. Later, Don told me the call was another of Jack's tests. I knew it was. Jack's tests were my pleasures. The drive allowed me to be alone with him for hours. He would talk and I would learn.

Here on the mountain we were alone again. I shouted into the cloudless sky, "I want to give you more, you son-of-a-bitch. Call me. Come back!!!"

Starting up the final incline to the ridge, I continued ranting. "Remember our nights without women" recalling nights when our wives were away and we camped at the studio and took care of the kids. There was one rare night in particular when everything, the company, the place, the light, temperature, food, smells, the colors, combined in harmony. It was not a great or monumental moment in time, just a glimpse of absolute perfection.

Now reaching the top, I stopped and shouted. "This is as far as I can go. Stay with me, Buddy. Help me work this out." It was then when the ocean came into view and I knew I was not alone, that he'd always be there for me in the clear air, the mountains, and tall grasses bending before the wind to "help me with my thinking," as he prefaced most advice. I'd hoped we could have gone on forever yet knew it couldn't be. Jack was dead.

I turned and began to run back down, then stopped and looked back, realizing I'd made a mistake. "I'm not leaving you up here, Old Friend. Come on and run with me." And he did. Jack was strong as an ox but not very athletic. We'd never run a step together before. Now he was at my side, running fast and light, as happy as I'd ever seen him.

My tears had dried when we ran under the train trestle at the bottom of the hill and reentered the campus. We'd been quietly enjoying each other's presence for many minutes by then.

Catching sight of a first group of students, Jack said, "I'm not going any further. See ya' later" and he was gone.

The Gym was empty when I returned. Afternoon classes had begun. I was exhausted. In the shower I felt peace in my chest where the pain had been. Our lives had been running on parallel tracks for ten years, nearly a fifth of his time alive. It was his gift to me, given without condition, and one I could never repay.

Magic & Loss

John Thomas, Electronic product manufacturer

His death wasn't too bad as deaths go—a morphine haze, dreams of his last trip to Paris in the sunlight, with short bouts of awareness. Requests for water, requests for friends, but mostly, just pleasant thoughts of trips, and memories, floating in and out of reality, or what we call reality when someone is lying in a hospital bed. Those were his final few weeks, days, and hours…stoned, fading away to a shell of his former self, dying and leaving us behind.

Losing him was bad as losses go, the loss of a friend, the loss of a sounding board, the loss of the magic that was John.

John was my wife's hairdresser. Yes, a fairly stereotypical hairdresser. Yes, my hairdresser also. John was also divorced, the father of two children, had two lovers while I knew him, and was best friend to many, if not all, of his clients.

As hairdressers go, John was ok. He cut my hair (the little I had left), and the hair of most of the people in my social group, not because he was a true star at his profession, but because he had the magic to make you feel for the fifteen to twenty minutes you were with him, that you were the most important person in his world and all was good in yours. No one ever departed from a session with John in a worse mood that when they came in. His laugh, his stories, his sense of humor, the glass of wine he served, all these things meant your day was better, your life was better. He loved us. I could feel it.

Over the course of our relationship, as I moved from being a client to a friend, John taught me many things. He taught me that I hate sailing. He taught me some really bad jokes that I still use to this day. He taught me that you can actually look cool in one of those Greek captain's sailing hats. Those things I may forget, but there were others I will never forget, lessons of his that changed my life.

John taught me to love and appreciate red wines. For this, I will think of him every time I pull a cork or enter my wine cellar. I enjoy the magic of finding a new wine that stops you in your tracks, forcing you to say, "Wow—that's good." And I enjoy sharing that wine, with my wife, my daughter, my friends, and my memories of John.

His passing taught me loss and the value of friendship. The loss of the magic that was John opened my eyes to that which is truly important in life. It helped me see for the first time that some things are beyond my control. That which I cherish can go away and not come back. My sense of manhood, my self-importance, my life and my world; were those equally elusive?

I am a man. I am serious. I am strong. I am stoic, often too busy to treat friends with the love they deserve. I show no emotions. I am a man. I have always acted that way, business first, wife second, friends & family third. When John disappeared from my life, I decided I could no longer think and behave that way. I could no longer let my life be second. I visited a few friends, all men, men that I respected, cared for, considered important in my life, men, like me, serious, self-contained. I scheduled appointments and appeared on time. I faced each one and told him, for the first time in our relationship, that he was my friend, someone important to me, a person that I loved and would miss terribly if he were gone. My sincerity overshadowed their universal astonishment and lack of defensive preparation for such an outpouring of affection. Together we quickly realized it was ok to tell someone you valued that you love them and need them in your life.

I am still a man. I'm often stupid, hardheaded, arrogant, and opinionated, especially when I forget the lessons from John. But now, I think I am a better man. I am sometimes more aware, more caring, more forgiving, more loving.

John, when you were alive I did not tell you that I loved you very often. I tell you now. I also tell others much more often now. The telling makes my life better. I try to live my life as you did. I try to be a good man, a good husband, a good father, a good son, and a good friend. But mostly I try to let those I love know that I love them. This is a lesson I learned from you, this is a lesson I need to remember, this is a lesson I need to teach my new grandchild.

John, I needed you in my life these past few years, I needed your wisdom, your help, your laugh. You could have helped me with some decisions I made, both good and bad. It would have been really nice to have you as a source of an honest "no bullshit" opinion. It would have been nice for you to tell me that you loved me, even when I was being stupid or arrogant.

John, what I really need is to remember what you taught me—to love red wine, to know that loss is forever, and to recognize and hold on to that which is special. And what is special to me is my wife, my family, my friends, my soon-to-be-arriving grandchild, and all that they bring to my life.

John, I hope Paris is sunny now, and for all your visits there.

Part Three:

Me and Them

It should be no surprise that men, in their struggle to satisfy their inherited duty to protect and provide, would expect to dominate in male-female relationships. Yet, within our increasingly egalitarian society, where rules have changed and women liberated, a confused male often finds himself engaged in a quixotic battle with windmills. With fewer winners and multitudes of losers being recorded, long, happy marriages have become increasingly rare.

Read how four men, decades apart in age, respond to individual problems of gender coexistence in typical manly terms.

In Passing

Gil Cooke, Architect, School Administrator

I'll never forget the day I left home for college at the too-young age of sixteen. My mom, who rarely gave advice, said, "Whatever you do, don't ever marry a girl that you can't say 'shit' in front of." Now that was sage parental counsel.

I listened well, paid heed; thought things were progressing nicely, but still wound up with the short end of the stick. Henny Youngman said it best with the line, "I had eleven good years of marriage and eleven out of twenty-six ain't that bad." Of course my ex might argue that only four of those years were good, but it's subjective and furthermore, I only had a twenty-five year warranty and figure I actually came out slightly ahead.

I can clearly recall the angst we both endured before making the 'big announcement' to our two early twenty-ish sons. We thought they'd be devastated. They weren't. Not a tear was shed. The oldest said, "Gee, that's too bad. Well, I'm off to band practice." The other said, "Yeah. That's the breaks" and also left. We were stunned. The following morning, when I cornered my younger son and asked him to share some feelings with me, he only added "For chrissake Dad, you should have gotten divorced years ago." In retrospect, the divorce was the greatest gift my ex could have given me. One day I plan to muster the balls to tell her so.

There is a huge difference between overcoming a "failed relationship" and making the step into a totally different life alone. Far from what I anticipated, the separation was more of a release than a downer. The expected arguments and legal detritus never surfaced and lost friendships seemed normal when I pulled up roots and moved from the East Coast to California. My mother and youngest son followed suit.

So here I sit, calculating the economics of survival after being wiped out financially by my attorney ex-wife. comparing my future with the sun as it dissolves into the horizon, with a bit of envy for old friends, younger than I and already retired.

Then came the dawn of realizing how much I truly love my life. As an architect, I find myself surrounded by sensitive, creative people. I am living in a verdant, still un-crowded and unspoiled, part of our planet. Fresh opportunities present themselves daily.

Moreover, my new life is actually going quite well. I have an unbelievably wonderful relationship with a beautiful, brilliant, somewhat younger woman who is highly respected in a profession very different from mine.

It seems we were meant to be together. When I mentioned to her that I was writing a few paragraphs for some offbeat book about guys and guy things, she said, "No shit." ?

Ideally there should not be a men's movement but a gender transition movement; only the power of the women's movement necessitates the temporary corrective of a men's movement. **Warren Farrell, Ph.D.**, The Myth of Male Power Berkley Books, NY

Porky

Milt Mannix, Advertising agent, retired

Joey, hey Joey—pinch the nipple
an' get me a double and a brew.
Thanks, ahhh, damn they're all bitches:
but, what'a ya gonna do!
- You wanna hear this, yeah?
Well, I jus' don' get it.
We just get done wit the good thing.
I'm happy, you bet she's happy, right,
but, all-a-sudden, she says, "sit!"
'Sit?' I say, whas-zhat mean?
She wants conversation.
'Talk! Ah Jeeze,' I say.
'Dinna' I jus' give it good ta ya?
Chris'mas, YOUR orgasm took me all day.'

I mean, Joey—waitin', helpin' hur,
that's sensitive, Right?
Like Really considerate, huh?
Well, remindin' hur, that's startin' a fight.
Know what she comes up wit' next?

"Two thurds of the wurld is women!
Whas-zhat mean heh?
Mudder a sweet Jesus, where's she get this stuff?
Like, what's it even got ta do wit sex?
I tell hur, she's the one for me and for me, hey, one's enough.
This content hur? Make hur feel special?
Nah man, no way, hur neck glows red
She starts to shovin' an pokin' me.
So, I'm outta hur bed; ya hear, I'm outta bed!
An' whas-zhat supposed ta mean?
In a million, you're nevah gonna guess -
Never mind, don' even try;
She tells ME, and tells me -

"It isn't right!" then, she leers kinda sly.
So I ask hur, 'Now, wha-da-fug I dou?'
She rasps—"you know."
Joey, I don'; but, I'm feelin' the jerk,
cause now she's cold—harsh as ice in your eye, man!
She spits, "Only Twenty Per Cent of US have good paying work.
Much less have any real wealth.
We are the many with the least.
IN AFRICA there's a ritual with knives;
little girls get cut, they're made to scream for nothing!
All Women Give, all their lives."

After this, Joey, she went ballistic,
pitchin' pillows and statistics too.
So, I fall back on reason; I mean, what else?
'Leslie, com'on babe; you know I love you...
let's talk nice hon -'

"You don't want to talk," she shouts.
"You understand one thing above your pitellas,"
Joey, pitella, whas-zhat mean?
I still don't get what it's about.
So, reason's out, I figure, smooth talk hur,
she likes that—usually, she likes that.
No way, she's got bitter as death,
hur tone-a-voice it's like totally flat.
She demands—"Do YOU think it's fair?"
'What?' I scream back, "just answer—tell me,
tell me..." then, she demands: "YOU TELL ME!"
Now, I had it, I Gave Hur her orgasm.
Man,
an end all orgasm, made hur blind; set hur Free! then this...
So—all I can think-a is—'SO!'
besides, I'm damn angry now-
I hollar, 'Do it yourself!' "What?"
Go on...get your own orgasm, go Leslie Go!'

You know wha' she does?
She tells me, "I'm a Pill
and she's sick of my medicine,"
then she snickers tricky like and snaps, "ey Porky, 'bout that
orgasm,
I Will!"
Next, bam, she slams the fuggin' door,
'Now, Joey, WHAS-ZAT all supposed ta mean?'

Life is self-expression, intricate organized polarity. The manhood and womanhood which would make the most of life in service to others is a sublimated form of the best of self which leads the way to a long life-time of usefulness, happiness, health and peace. **Luther Burbank**, Why I Am an Infidel Haldeman-Julius Co. 1926

All men make mistakes, but married men find out about them sooner. **Red Skelton**

He knew the precise psychological moment when to say nothing. **Oscar Wilde** (The Portrait of Dorian Gray)

"Just as, from a girl's perspective, history books are filled with men, from a boy's perspective, school itself is filled with women. It is women teaching him how to be a boy by conforming to what women tell him to do after he's been trained to conform to what his mother tells him to do." **Warren Farrell** (The Myth of Male Power, Berkley Books)

Sing In Me Muse, And Through Me Tell The Story
Homage to Homer, The Odyssey
Steven Foster, Teen Program Director, mentor

The year I left graduate school (1965), my brother Greg gave me a book that changed my life. It was a translation of the Odyssey by Robert Fitzgerald. From the moment I opened this great legacy of our sacred ancestors, I was spellbound. Never after able to put it down, the story relentlessly sought me out and found me in the sacred chambers of memory—and thrust a tear-sword into my soul. I must have read it 50 times, and every time I wept and put it down—only to take it up again as time and exigency permitted. 2500 years of human history wouldn't let me go. Those years vanished the moment I re-read the first sentence. The story wasn't about the "good old days" when men heroically contended with the gods. It was about now—about me—about how it feels to be a man.

Forty years later, still longing for home, I take up the pen to write about The Odyssey. Forty years of wandering. Forty years of grief. Forty years behind the tiller on the open sea, drifting with the fickle winds and currents of life, contending, grieving, finding, losing. Forty years in the boudoirs of the witch. Forty years of lying, stealing, plundering, shape-shifting. Forty years of playing the fool. Forty years of nymphs and underworlds and passages and tests and comrades and ghosts. Forty years of trying to get back to my sons and daughters. Forty years of longing for my woman, for the secrets of our bed, and the ultimate fulfillment of home.

Now, all those years of wandering have coalesced into this Phaiákian ship with black sails, in which I lie at ease, looking up at the night sky, heart-heavy with the treasures of a lifetime of grief—no more than a few hours from the rocky slopes of Ithaka. Calmly, the crew goes about their collective task, setting and trimming the sail, steering by the beacon of the Great Wain. They too know the taste of disappointment and grief, and the ecstasy of waking up at dawn, their lovers by their side. Pale nymphs crowd around, seeing in me the man of their dreams. But I know better. No matter which goddess or god I slept with, I always knew what I really wanted. As sleep tugs at my eyes, I whisper a prayer under my breath to the woman who has made all the difference: "If I have been untrue, it was never to you."

Men sometimes speak well of me in the councils. I am content with that, and I know none of this approval will mean a blessed thing when, for the last time, I stand tall in the hall of the suitors and nock the arrow of destiny to the bowstring of life. The battles, the enchantments, the doldrums, the comrades brave and free, the truths and lies, the lonely years, will come to me in the here and now, and amount to nothing, if I cannot string the bow.

As the black ship, like "a four horse team, whipped into a run on a straightaway, shows her heels to the swell," I fall asleep. Despite all those days of breasting roads and waves, my mind is finally at rest. Soon I will land on my rocky island home. A great struggle awaits me there. Before the gates of death I will fight the good fight. When and if the battle is won, I will enter the secret of the bed. And then I will carry my oar far away from the ocean of life.

One last time I will take a stand against those karmic monsters who threaten my homecoming, knowing full well they are my just deserts. Long ago I decided to go off to the war. I could have said no. I could have convinced those who called me that I truly was insane. No doubt I was, or believed myself to be, as I plowed the beach and sowed my salt. But I couldn't resist the call. I had to learn that such decisions have consequences, not the least of which were grievous troubles, murderous dangers, and separation from those I loved the most.

How many times, drifting in the "solid deep-sea swell, awaiting death," did I mindlessly boast about my prowess to the god of earthquakes? This macho vainglory gave me nothing but heartache. Again and again the Earthshaker moved against me: "Go on, go on, wander the high seas this way, take your blows, before you join that race the gods have nurtured. Nor will you grumble, even then, I think, for want of trouble."

But for now, "slumber, soft and deep, like the still sleep of death, closes my eyes, as the ship heaves seaward." A goddess watches over me. Somehow I always knew it. She has been there all along, even in extremity, and has helped me through innumerable crises. I keep complaining to her, "Where are you when I need you?" Do I complain to her, or to myself? "Rag of a man that

I am, is this the end of me? I fear the goddess told it all too well—predicting great adversity at sea and far from home. Now all things bear her out."

Blessed slumber falls like a starry night. There's nothing I can do but surrender to Muse of Dreams. In my gut I know she will convey me to the lands where dreams forget.

Sing in me Muse.

> A man who has been in touch with his feelings all his life will usually avoid a midlife crisis. But a man who has denied his feelings all his life, and then learns to get in touch with them in middle age, will precipitate a midlife crisis. Which is not necessarily a bad thing. If he's precipitating a midlife crisis among people who love him, it can be the first time in his adult life he feels loved for something other than being a wallet. Then he has a chance of directing the movie of his life rather than being the jerk of his life. **Warren Farrell, Ph.D**; Women Can't Hear What Men Don't Say; Tarcher/Putnam, 1999

Another Goodbye

Josef Kasperovich, Photographer

Pick your poison, draw the card.
What is it makes this life so hard?
I'll let myself out the way I came,
And close the door like nothing's changed.

Sun goes down on a distant hill.
I ride towards it even still.
I try to reach and touch its glow,
But its chilling embers are all I'll know.

It's often hard to start things slow.
At least the voices tell me so.
Is it in your heart or in your head?
Is it in the kitchen or in the bed?

Please tell me again who sent you my way.
Was it the Angels, did they hear me pray?
If they were bringing love, why'd they wait so long,
And did they mean to leave me with this song?

This could have been the sweetest thing.
A man, a woman and then a ring.
Love that's meant to last all time.
I guess that time's just in our mind.

I've gotten good at these good-byes,
Though even now I can still cry.
You must admit we stood a chance.
I only wish you hadn't left the dance.

Go your way and I'll go mine.
It will get easier with time.
And after all is said and done.
No one's lost, but no one's won.

CENTERFOLD

Roberto Armstrong, unassuming, middle-aged, soft-spoken sculptor, painter, and college teacher of English as a second language, offers a humorous manly spin on Creationism

Jehovah Gives Witness

Roberto Armstrong, Professor of English, artist, poet

You know Me.
I'm the One who made
Humankind and birds.
(And don't forget their turds!)
Master of light and shade
I grew…
Just for you…
The tree.
See!
Inventor of the penis
I made semen
(and pee)
And Eve, My Venus.
I'm the He-man
Who says it's lewd
To get screwed
Unless you marry.
I harry

With threats
Of hellfire's burning
If you place your bets
On roulettes
Turning.

That's Good Old Me, too,
Who
Saves sinners,
Backs winners,
Dumps losers,
Wobbles boozers,
Weighs your pluses and minuses,
Blocks your sinuses,
Prescribes a wonder pill
(You call it freedom of the will.)
On condition you don't use it
'Cause you're certain to abuse it.
Yes, that's Me,
Dear Old Me
Strong and Free

Your loving Father,
Though I do hate the bother
Of endlessly hugging
My earthly progeny.
It's not homophobia or misogyny.
I'm just tired of their bugging
Me.

Can I help it if My Tastes
Run to scaring?
There's not as much fun in caring.
It wastes
The time I'd rather spend
On hellfire and damnation.
(You'll get your ration
With the world's end!)

To clear up the mystery,
Here's some of My History.
I started out small
With a thunderous call
To the Jews
Who were few but ambitious,
To give up their vicious,
Seditious-
ly primitive views.
In return for their smites
At those smarmy Do-rites
And those haughty Upptites
I'd choose the Semites.
But first they'd have
To make a stab
At pleasing Me, Jehovah.
(Aren't I allowed a little fun?)
They'd prove that their subjection
Was more than genuflection,
By sacrificing Abraham's son
And I'd be Number One
When it was over.

In the event
I chose to relent
Just to show the snide
My Kinder Side.
But if they thought
I could be bought
Or they could flee
From their guarantee
Or from Omniscient Me,
Citing chapter and verse
I threatened to curse
And shower disgrace
On my chosen race
For ever
And ever.

The Jews in My Pocket,
I was onto bigger game.
The Christians were next on My Docket
Then came
Islam.
But just when I thought
I'd settled their lot
They threw Me a bomb
The beggars sought to call Me Allah,
As if I were just any old fella!
When they captured My Holy City
I sent my minions
Out of pity
To make them pay
For their opinions
Sad to say,

I couldn't sway their thinking
Much less goad
Them into blinking,
Even after thousands died
And their stinking
Bodies lay
Side by side
Along the road.

As for my believers
(those over-achievers!)
However absurd or far-out
The demands I would send
To make them all bend
And submit to My Clout,
They would do it tout de suite
With tribute replete
In supine fear of My Knout.
Sadly,
There were and there are
Too many of those
Who chose
Gladly
(I say badly.)
To follow a different star,
Or…
And this is still worse…
To seek within
(A terrible sin!)
For the sight
Of some light
In their dark universe.
I give them My Curse!

But Up Here I'm different.
I'm warm and forgiving.
I'm well concupiscent!
And I'm into High Living,
As My Elected can see
Arrayed next to me
On my couch here in Heaven.
No, they can't miss the leaven-
ing of My Marvelous Member
Which I richly deploy
And the Saved all enjoy
No matter their gender.

I'm sure you're in shock
At My Pride in My Cock,
Aghast at My Bi-sexual Flings,
Though my Holy Book praises
As Heavenly the Embraces
Of Me, your King of Kings.
Perhaps you thought
My love could be got
Like your magicians' arts,
And without private parts.
But I made man to look like I do,
And it would have been callous
To leave out his phallus,
And he would have been jealous,
(You'll agree that is true),
though, compared to My Own,
his is only a drone,
A poor little clone,
When you look at the Giant

With which I'm endowed,
So awesomely pliant
And proud.

Still, I threaten jails
For earthly males
Who stick theirs in
Their male kin,
Or use their lips
To suck those rich-
And febrile tips or tickle bungs
With agile tongues.
(All of which
Are Heavenly trips!)
As for the girls,
It's endless whirls
On the rungs
Of My Royal Ladder.
It doesn't hurt them in the least
Though it reaches to their bladder.
And when I fill them,
West and East,
With My Paradisiacal Jism
They all implore,
"More!"
And I'm quick to please 'em.

Down on Earth it's
Another story.
Mixing fear with flits]of glory
Suits My Aim
For humankind.
To maim

And bind
Their pleasures
With measures
Designed
To hem them in
And make a sin
Of what Up Here
Is sheer
And total bliss
Is not remiss
But mere
Commonsense
Seen through My Lens.
Thus I deny to a miss
But allow to a missus
Some joys of the senses
(though not in their menses).
And however delicious,
I outlawed fellation
As vicious,
For fucking
Not sucking
Promotes procreation!
No condoms or birth controls either.
I will sanction no breather
For My harried race
To slow the pace
Of their frightened dash
To Salvation,
Though it's all a great bash
For Me
As you'll see.
Whoopedee!

My Premiere Creation,
Eve, was made by Me
Out of sheer elation.
In a fit of inspiration
I could plainly see
I needed something round and plush
To fill My Hands (and give as rush
To cock and brain!), a place of rest
No! Two!...I'd make a breast
For each. And as a treat...
Applaud My Feat!...
To let My Fingers ripple
As they please
With horny zest
Or sensuous ease
I added a nipple
That I could also suck or squeeze!
It would set her juices running
Though this was just a tease,
A mini-sample of My Cunning.
To give fullness to My Work of Art,
To lend it heart
To give it depth and soul,
I envisioned a deep hole
Warm and slick and lush,
And hedged above by hairy brush.
Here, at last,
An irresistible confection
To house what in the past
Had been My useless Godly Erection.
(Well, not entirely so.
I had pulled It to and fro

And shot My Juices high and low.)
And though
I came too fast
On our first connection,
It aroused her from her slumber,
And she begged Me for more lumber,
And to try to make it last
Much longer
And stronger.

We went at it day and night
Until, one day, in fright,
She pointed to her welling girth.
It seems My Endless Sperm
Contained the germ
Of birth.
Rats!
This wasn't what I had in mind:
To interrupt our pleasure
To care for bawling brats
Or sacrifice My Treasure
To make others of My Kind.
But I'm not God for nothing
So I passed My Fertile, Frothing
Sperm to man
To make as he can.
(My clever little servant
Turned out to be observant
And devised ways of averting
The products of his spurting!)

But this is to get ahead
Of the story you have read.
Your story goes that I
Made Adam out of clay
And Eve of Adam's rib.
If I may
I'd like to give
That unimaginative fib
The lie.
Adam didn't live
Until I first
In a wanton burst
Of Creative Pride
Made Eve,
Glorious Eve,
Her juicy girth
Not from earth,
But from My Hide.
And not just any part
But from what I most prize,
For the greatest art
Is the child of sacrifice.
Yes, you guessed,
I made My Eve, My Venus
With the flesh of My Godly Penis!

But later came the painful test
Of what to do
When she got pregnant.
Can the One Regnant
Have a mate
(or two)

to share His Fate?
She might come to think
She was His equal.
And in the sequel
Would she shrink
From driving Him to drink
By claiming her rights
In rancorous fights?
There had to be a way out,
Something new,
Where I could use My Clout
To let Me have My Cake
And eat It, too.
For I'd gotten used to sex
And had to slake
My Appetite and to ex-
Press, with cocksman's thrust
And tongue and fingers' flex
My Never-ending Lust
For flesh.
It was a mess,
But I am blessed
With inventive vision
And great precision
In putting unheard of things together.
Still, I was near the end of My Tether
When I finally came to My Decision:
My dear, voluptuous Eve
Would have to leave
And descend to Earth
To face rebirth,
But in such a way,

At the end of the day
(or the hour...
it was for Me to say)
She would gladly come back
And jump in the sack
Or lustily roll in a bower
Of hay,
But lay
No claim to My Power.

I had to act quickly
For Eve was quite sickly
I could hardly get near
Without a complaint
That she'd faint
If My Engine got in her.
It was while I was whacking
My Invincible Cock
And planning Eve's packing
That I took stock
And saw what was lacking.
There he was...I had him!...
His outlines fair
On My Love-King Bare....
It was Adam!

To make him real
I would have to peel
A substantial layer
Off My Indomitable Player,
This proof of My Genius
No small inconvenience.

Temporarily marred
By this surgical blow
It would hurt when hard
For a week or so,
While down on earth,
Adam's home at birth,
My Sumptuous Eve
Breasts aswell,
Would quickly weave
Her magic spell.
Lured to that Grail
(that was made for My Rail),
Adam's lance would upheave
And they'd cleave
The one to the other
When Eve had Cain
It would cause no strain
For Adam to believe
He'd made her conceive
Though Eve was already a mother.

Just when it seemed
Their life was a dream
I sent to Adam
And to his madam
And to all their line
(They were all really mine!)
My Godly Directive
It was loaded with invective
And with righteous indignation
At their human dissipation.
They had taken as their treasure

The life of sensual pleasure
But they'd forgotten the Divine.
Now they'd have to quell
This appetite for Hell
(another idea of mine
I'd designed to spell
An end to their illusion.)
They were certain to quake
When they heard My Conclusion
To damn them pell-mell
If they tried to break
My Commands, or rebel.
In stark contrast
I temptingly painted
For those who had fainted
From fear at My Blast
Visions of bliss
To reward the untainted.
If they followed My Rules
There was no way to miss
Getting pools
Of jewels
When they died.
And I subtly implied
There were secret delights
That would fill their nights.
(I haven't lied.)

Mixing guilt with sex
I aimed not just to vex
But to fuel their desire

So I could reap its fire.
Thus, whatever the season,
If for no obvious reason,
You see Me quaking with pleasure,
It's because there's a pair
Here or there
Anywhere,
Who are shar-
ing the Gift of My Treasure.
And though it may make you sore,
I also adore
(as I told you before),
What Adam does with Steve
Or Caroline with Eve.
(And what you do alone
Is equally prone
To dazzle My Bone.)
Yes, each guilty spasm
Of each human orgasm
Sparks the Mystical Surge
The Heavenly Splurge,
Of My Holy Ghost.
(That's no idle boast!)

But for My Chosen Few
It's an unsettling preview
A delicious pre-taste
(unless there's a waste!…
They did it in haste)
Of the Feast of Love
That awaits them Above.

So they owe a toast
To their beneficent Host
Who's taught a lesson or two
To your modern ad-men,
Those penultimate mad-men,
About balancing strictures
With beautiful pictures
Of fun things to do.

But enough talk of sex.
There's more to My Genius
Than inserting My Penis
In Geena.
(Or Rex.)
I reject, too, the rumor
That I've no sense of humor.
It's grown like a tumor
But it's surely a jest.
For I'm quite fest-
ive and I can attest,
That I've made giraffes
Just for the laughs.
And while some may think
(Not those in the pink!)
My humor's black
Because of My Knack
For giving cancers
To ballroom dancers
And grizzled ranchers
(And all kinds of others,
Like fathers and mothers

And sisters and brothers)
The Bible shows I'm not a quack.

And, of course,
You all want to know
If I show remorse
When innocents cry
And I let them die.
Don't dare even ask
Or take Me to task!
My ways are inscrutable,
Never disputable,
As mysterious to Me
As to those who see
Only dog eat dog
In the mutable
Lexicological fog.
(But here's an aside
At some cost to My Pride
That's somewhat disturbing
And might cause some curbing
Of your confidence
In My Omnipotence:
For I must tell you I view
My Life as a question.
If I made you
And the old and the new,
What I can't see
Is <u>Who</u> made Me?
Do you have a suggestion?)

(It's an infinite regression
That could lead to depression
And such
If I thought about it much.
But, I don't
And I won't
Because if I do
I could be through.
Then, too
It's still great fun
To keep My fans on the run.
And while the sex stays great,
I won't question My Fate.
Would you?)

Part Four:

It's a Dick Thing!

In spite of a currently popular metaphor which generalizes males as angry aggressors and females as loving peacemakers, any fair analysis shows that people are people; that within their individual struggles to attain balance in their lives, both men and women can be described as being akin to Mars and/or Venus at one time or another.

Look beneath an often hard, defensive crust and discover that men are neither more nor less human than other brainy members of the animal kingdom. To wit, the following five separate, yet typically male viewpoints attest.

Heat of the Moment

Dana Jones, Computer Consultant, provocateur

It was the last weekend of June 1989—a chilly summer day in San Francisco. Chuck and I had made plans to rendezvous at the Castro Street MUNI stop to make the underground voyage to the vortex of depravity—the annual Gay Pride Parade. Accompanying

75

us on our adventure was Denise; my then girlfriend, our voice of conscience, and occasionally, the enforcer when we transgressed appropriate behavioral limits.

Our goal was to establish ourselves curbside (with folding lawn chairs) on Market Street in time for the traditional opening of the parade—Dykes on Bikes—an assembly of motorcycling lesbians on every conceivable bike; from measly moped to full-dress hog.

A few hours later, when the bulk of the procession had passed, we began wandering through the crowd toward the Civic Center where booths vending the rainbow debris and sub-cultural iconography of the gay experience awaited us.

Shortly after our arrival in the central plaza, Denise noticed a yellow tent on the North side of the plaza with an extremely long line snaking out from the structure and out into the barrier-blocked street.

A "bit" part in Dick, the latest film project undertaken by documentary filmmaker Jo Menell, lured the standees, all men, into waiting for the first second of the 15 minutes of fame promised by pop artist Andy Warhol. Menell's documentary-in-progress was to be a women's perspective on the male appendage.

As Chuck and I approached the line in an effort to determine the ground rules—the standard disclaimers that you would expect—you agree to have your likeness used in the film, you agree to forego monetary compensation—Denise piped up with the challenge. "Why don't you guys do it"?

Of course! Who wouldn't stand in line for an hour for the opportunity to drop their pants in front of a stranger's camera? The gauntlet had been thrown down—by the voice of sobriety and reason, no less.

As Chuck and I joined the line and signed away our rights, I began to absorb the complete scene. There were about 300 men in the line ahead. The demographic was solidly gay—no surprise there. At the front of the line I noticed that the skirt of the tent ended about a foot above grade level enabling passersby to observe the participants' pants bunch around their ankles prior to and during the photo shoot. Nice touch.

The would-be participants had that contagious exuberance that accompanies the expectation of a naughty deed. Chuck and I joked about the situation beaming as the people passing by realized our purpose. We attempted to recruit strangers to our new-found cause with the zealotry of Pat Robertson on a pilgrimage through Sodom. Our conversion rate proved to be no better than what Pat would have expected.

Chuck and I had been in line for about an hour. As we approached the front of the line (about 30 guys ahead of us) I noticed a disturbing trend—attrition from the ranks. It seems that some of our compatriots were losing their nerve as they approached the inner sanctum of the tent. What would it be that could deter them from such an honorable mission with success so near at hand?

As my moment of celebrity approached I was beset by some anxieties—perhaps the same anxieties that deterred my comrades. My section of the line had moved into the shadow cast by the tent and the air had become somewhat chilly which led to obviously unwanted involuntary contractions. Additionally, I became aware that my clothing choice, confining, compacting briefs instead loose-fitting, expansive boxers, would hamper my ability to recover in stealth. With time racing on—a tactical plan needed immediately. I was going on record for God's sake! How would I measure up?

Hands in my pockets pretending to search for change, I attended to the situation as best I could. Though Levi pockets aren't really designed for adjustments of the scale required, I was able to manage a bit of extra comfort room. Now tenth in line, I decided that it wasn't appropriate to reach into my briefs to open up any additional real estate. As you might expect, the men at the head of the line were receiving the most scrutiny from the crowd and I didn't want to appear either perverted or vain.

Suddenly, another thought occurred to me. In all likelihood, I would soon be exposing myself to the scrutiny of a gay man—a detail that had somehow escaped me in the rush to participate. Did this somehow compromise my heterosexual credentials? I decided it did not. Anyway, it was already too late.

I was first in line. Chuck had dropped back and let me take the lead. Thanks, Chuck, old buddy.

Inside the tent it was strictly professional: a Hasselblad portrait camera on a tripod at crotch level; next to it a high-end Polaroid on a separate tripod. The photographer—of indiscernible gender preference—politely asked me to drop my pants. I complied, glancing down. "Clearly not my best showing," I thought wistfully, adding "still not my worst either."

The photographer snaps a Polaroid and gives me the photo as a souvenir. (This will prove an invaluable means of identification a few months hence when I purchase the home video).

In preparation for the definitive Hasselblad shot, I became increasingly aware that the summer chill was beginning to reclaim its physiological victory. I did my best to think warm, mildly prurient thoughts until I was officially photographed, thanked and excused.

Cut forward two months to the gala premier of "Dick" the 15-minute documentary at the Castro Theater.

The ticket line cascades down the entire block and around the corner. The poster boasts "100 women interviewed, 1,000 dicks exposed."

Theater management has even opened the rarely used balcony to allow extra capacity.

Denise has accompanied Chuck and me for our big screen debut.

As the film opens, a stream of black and white close up images accosts the audience while the 'interviewed women' answer a series of questions. "What do male appendages remind you of?"

"Would you want one?"

"What about your first experience with one?"

"Does size matter?" "How can you tell?"

"What do you think that men think?"

The juxtaposition of the startling variance in the photographic subjects (1000 wide-screen dicks ÷ (15 minutes @60 seconds/minute) = 1.11 dicks/second) and the dispassionate narrative of the interviewees ("looks like a vacuum cleaner hose") easily captured the audience. Gasps and guffaws erupted at the subjects' sundry adornments, felt-penned attachments—messages and modifications—a piercing here, a padlock there.

Finally, as the credits roll, alphabetically listing the names and pseudonyms of the cast, cheers from secular friends and family burst from groups of fans throughout the theater. We were the bold, born of a proud gender, fearlessly displaying the proof of our claim to manhood, for that moment and for the rest of history.

VIAGRACIAS!

Ray Clark Dickson, Poet

Oh, to rise in jubilation
for what hath risen!
A new day, flesh saluting sky
where birds are singing,
joy delirious, unconstrained;
time when a throb in the veins
does more than linger, live
performances, once again,
are sweetening the hay.

"Mr. T"

William Stansfield, Professor of Biology, retired

Girl baby says to boy baby:
"Are you a boy or a girl?"
Boy baby: "I'm a boy."
Girl baby: "How can you tell?"
Boy baby: "Look under my blanket. My booties are blue."

Yeah, we males are different from females right from the get go. These differences are mainly due to nature (heredity) and nurture (family and cultural environments) over which we had no control. At puberty, the testes go into overdrive with production of testosterone, resulting in sperm production, increased facial and body hair, lower pitched voice, development of upper body strength, and elevated muscle to fat ratio.

Testosterone also creates behavioral/psychological changes. Studies indicate that male children tend to be more hyperactive than females and show a greater adventurous sense of curiosity and exploratory behavior in new situations. Many a male ego is based on contributions that adventurous and curious men have made to society. We glory in how great it is to live the life of a man, but too many of us do so with very little appreciation of how much prejudice, inconvenience, psychological trauma, physical discomfort and pain we have escaped by being born male rather than female.

Men, of course, have problems of their own. Some men have a gene for baldness that, with age, becomes activated by even standard levels of testosterone. Other more serious long-term effects of testosterone include possible heart disease, susceptibility to infection, enlargement of the prostate gland, and a host of other maladies. Biologically speaking, like it or not, men are the "weaker sex" in this regard, which might also explain part of the difference in male/female life spans. Testosterone levels tend to become elevated when men participate in sports (often just by watching sports) and in confrontational situations where guys might throw a punch before trying to settle a dispute in a less aggressive manner. Men are much more likely than women to be involved in violent crime. It is probably true that many men have to consciously override their aggressiveness to fit into polite society, an aspect of maleness usually impossible for women to comprehend. These aggressive tendencies sometimes lead men to pursue vocations that demand placing their lives on the line. One of the factors that prompted me to write this article was the recent death of Dale Earnhardt on the final lap of the Daytona 500. Recognized as America's greatest active racecar driver, he died at age 49. But men all too often put themselves in danger just for the excitement of it. Mountain climbers, bungee jumpers, bobsled racers, sky and deep sea divers, etc. apparently place a higher value on "a thrill" than they do about their own lives or the concerns of those who love them. Testosterone probably plays a large part in dulling men's sense of values in this regard. If we allow it, testosterone can kill us.

Remember the former bouncer and actor who played "Mr. T" on "The A Team?" He is a guy who obviously has enough testosterone (hence his name?). Some body-builders and athletes take anabolic steroids (like testosterone) to attain strength and muscular physiques. However, it is not nice to fool Mother Nature and some of these guys pay a heavy price. The pro wrestler Hulk Hogan was seen on TV warning us about the abuse of such drugs. At the time he was a very sick man with a bad prognosis. How vainly macho can men be? Very, very vain indeed! So what if you don't have a muscular build or a full head of hair? Any person (male or female) you'd choose for a friend wouldn't care about your testosterone level or your physical appearance; they'd like you for your inner qualities, your compassion and generosity, your faithfulness to a set of moral standards, and your courage in the face of adversity. Yeah, we're different from women and we each have gender problems to contend with. Let's just recognize and respect these differences as equal partners in the game of life and move on to make whatever contributions we can to a better world.

The Wild Man

In *Iron John, A Book About Men* (Vintage/Random, 1990), **Robert Bly** writes of the "Wild Man" as an inherent precept of manly virility and strength and warns against attempting to become the beast and unleash destruction on self and society as opposed to being "in touch with" it to savor the sensation.

Fruitcakes

Don Koberg, Professor, Emeritus (Architecture)

The Odd Fellows' Hall was jammed belly to belly with pre-Mardi Gras revelers tuning up for Fat Tuesday still two weeks off. There were the usual sequins, beads and a few masks, but our costumes and makeup were special. Along with the band and Cajun eats, we'd been touted as the feature of the evening's entertainment.

Once the decision had been made to put on another show and word of what we were planning got around, we were committed. We were truly funny and milking it for all it was worth. That's all that mattered. I can't remember having ever laughed harder at myself in my entire life.

More than burly men clowning around in thrift shop dresses, ratty wigs, and overstuffed brassieres, we were Hollywood quality sluts, five guys decked out like Kit Kat girls from our 'ho-heels' and fishnet stockings to false eyelashes, flaunting everything we could muster to look sexy and preparing to go on stage as the brazen hussies of *Cabaret*.

Mike McGee, six foot three, ex-French Quarter bartender and one time offshore oil rigger, was Helga. Joe, six two, bass-voiced middle member of the brothers Empey and Pub Irish to the core, was Mausy while Mark 'Five hundred push-ups before breakfast' Jorgesen, aped 'cute as a button' Heidi. George, with copper bangs, bee stung lips and sailor hat, and bald me, in blond curls and cocky derby, belied our status as group elders pushing seventy. In our pink and green satin shorts with sequined crotch, we completed the chorus line as Christina and Inga.

This wasn't our virgin appearance. Four successful years performing skits from *Let's Misbehave*, *Mickey's Monkey*, *Ray Charles and The Rayettes*, and *The Village People* had us believing that we were getting good at bending the perceptions of our audience. This was to be our finest fifteen minutes of fame.

Few words were exchanged as we passed through the crowd heading toward the stage. But, the looks we got you wouldn't believe. Even close pals, buddies we'd known for years of butting heads on the scrimmage line of life, were stupefied by our appearance. Their wide-eyed stares and mouths agape asked the obvious question loud and clear: "How could you betray us and our shared manliness by dressing like fruitcakes and prancing around like sissies?"

We couldn't have cared less. Homophobic hogwash no longer made any difference to we who were savoring the joy of changing sides and viewing our gender with fresh eyes. We were right in having fun as men dressed up like women and we knew it. The proof was in the envy we sensed existing behind every sneer, snicker, and muffled belly laugh directed our way.

Weeks later, make that months, now more than a year, all five of us look back on that night when the hall darkened, the din hushed, the curtain parted, and the limelight focused on Stuart, the gay emcee host of The Kit Kat Club and a spitting image of Joel Gray in his tails and Clown White greasepaint. He and Debbie, our choreographer-costumer, male and female coaches working together with instant understanding and without a hitch, had taught us so much in the short period of five dinner/rehearsals. With Stuart leading the way and Debbie in the wings calling the shots, our initial vulgar clumsiness had slowly softened to almost harmonize with their natural smoothness. No matter how hard we tried to stretch our socially imposed manly limits and feign sexiness, we would never come close to being as convincingly 'fraulein' as either of them. Our long practiced robotic style would overshadow every twist and kick.

A threat to compromising our sexuality was never an issue for us. Our eyes clarified our preferences from the start, all five pair of them, windows to lustful souls, glued to every sensual movement of Debbie's leotard from the first rehearsal to show time. Only those die-hard defenders of machismo, guys who would never dare to risk their manly image, were intimidated by our shenanigans.

Why it is that a man in tights can frighten so many, yet appear hilarious to so many others is a paradox I'm not qualified to explain. Warriors throughout history, from gallant knights and murderous Crusaders to modern day wrestlers, all wear them. One thing I do know for sure: whenever I venture out of the box labeled *For Men Only*, I enter a realm where the differences between male and female, both straight and gay are almost understandable. I go to play and inevitably stay to learn.

C'mon man, just because a guy goes onstage wearing a dress and makeup it doesn't mean he's light in his loafers. Does it?

Like a Man!!?
Stand up and Fight like a man!
Take it and Die like a man!
Gird up now thy loins like a man! (Job, 38:3)
Be a mensch!

Revision

Steven deLuque, Painter, baker

It was the accumulated tonnage of decades of life's experiences that balanced uncomfortably on George's shoulders. Poundage acquired by the suicide of his best friend when he was 16, the death of his mother on his thirtieth birthday (the real surprise at his surprise party), and the unwelcome joy of his marriage to Wanda. Tonnage that now, like an oxen's yoke, accelerated the force of gravity making it nearly impossible to put one foot in front of the other so that he could reach the bathroom in time to avoid pissing himself.

George's bladder was stretched and aching, each unsteady step accentuating its fullness. The hallway stretched interminably.

Jesus, whoever planned a house with the bathroom so far from the bedroom?

George reached it just in time, pulling up the leg of his stained boxer shorts and letting the stream flow. Having a good piss was just about the greatest physical pleasure in George's hectic and disordered life.

Masturbating had lost its thrill after Wanda's death four years ago. After her death, George's penis had become strictly utilitarian; its small, wrinkled, tubular form no longer performing in even the perfunctory morning hard-on. It wasn't the kind of penis to envy, more likely to cause ennui. George had always been bemused by its ordinariness. Wanda had acted as if it was the staff of life. But then she had been a virgin on their wedding night and had nothing with which to compare it. Well, George had been a virgin also if you didn't count the homoerotic explorations of adolescence.

Alright, alright; there had been Paul in college. Two years with Paul, whenever they both had been so drunk that, the next day, they could conveniently forget how good the sex had been or even that they had engaged in mutual cock-sucking. Even with Paul the size of George's penis had failed in comparison. But, back then, it had never failed in performance. It was always ready at the utterance of the slightest sexual innuendo or at the most furtive brushing of anyone's hand. It was instantly turgid and anxious. The exuberance of youth still a fond memory.

George stared at his reflection in the mirror above the sink, the countenance of an older, defeated man halfheartedly returning his stare. The eyes drooped, the jowls sagged, the chin weakened, the hairline receded. What had happened to all those years? The years had been traded, one for one, for pounds; the hair, by the same ratio, for wrinkles. The physical now interfered with the intellectual, how could one think when discomfort was constant?

George, his head aching, tottered down the hall, back to the bedroom, and climbed back between the cotton sheets weighted by the thick down comforter.

I can rest another hour or so to ease this hangover, that will give me a couple of hours to straighten the house before starting dinner. God, when was the last time I wanted to cook dinner?

Paul stirred next to him, lightly snoring, his insistent erection pressing into George's thigh. They had had far too much to drink at the class reunion yesterday. Neither would be able to remember much, if anything, of the previous night.

Me

Steve Omega, Wanderer

You know I don't bitch when things aren't perfect. I don't whine about a pain or a big bill or something going wrong with the car. When I'm in trouble nobody knows. If something needs taking care of, or a bit of criminality needs doing, then I don't go round up everyone I know asking for them to agree with me. I just get on with it.

If someone needs something, I do my best to provide it. Not just pulling out the wallet, but the time to get them their desire, which once accomplished, quickly translates into some other priority.

Why am I like this?

Because I'm a man.

Whatever

Robert O'Brien, Retail Sales Manager

In-out. Up-down, forward or backward. Yin and yang. All are extremes that represent either side of the equation. Men and women.

When women get together and "Ya Ya" or yap about a monologue with their vagina or do "the chick thing" they are more than likely fulfilling some void in the cosmos. Some do the blame game by pointing painted fingernails at men or other women they find threatening to their shaky constitution. And some laugh all the way to the bank.

Likewise when men gather and beat on sticks or otherwise break the silence between them (Jesus Christ, MEN CAN'T HEAR WHAT MEN DON'T SAY!) they are gravitating toward fulfilling some void in the cosmos. Some blame women for their ills or try to undermine their peers with dishonesty rationalized as "rules of the jungle." And some crawl back under a car or whack some ball around on a golf course or even take it to the bank.

Who cares? What comes out of this is that both genders are searching for some meaning in their life. William Blake wrote that when you seek the soul in you, your soul will, in turn, look toward you. That, my friend, is a new order of self-esteem!

This is not a culture that prides itself on meaningfulness. Heroes in America are on a need to know basis. When I hitch up my pants by the belt loops or puff out my chest or get my panties all in a bunch, am I performing some elaborate courting dance? Does any of this gender sidling mean anything more than posturing? I think not. Finding your soul or your desire or whatever you want to call it is on a case-by-case basis.

Get humble. Get clear. Get going.

Men are from Earth. Women are from Earth. Deal with it!
(Anon.)

PART FIVE:

SECRETS

If, as Human Studies reveal, women can't hear what men don't say, it's also true that silent men are also denied knowing what is truly in their hearts and minds. Of course, when it comes to the telling and/or keeping of secrets, the odds for spreading the news tend to favor the most talkative. It's not so much that men are better secret-keepers than women but that remaining silent is a man's proven method of non-aggressive self-protection.

Here, with their defenses down and innermost thoughts and fears bared for all to see, witness the true manly gestures of five brave souls.

Truth Telling Is the Best Aphrodisiac

Bob Banner, Window washer, publisher

At one time there used to be models, rules and various guidelines that helped us define what it meant to be "in a relationship." There was a consensual agreement and a security in knowing the rules; knowing what was expected of us. But today the guidelines are no longer tidy and well scripted. And that can breed much insecurity let alone confusion and frustration. Yet this same insecurity can also be viewed as most challenging because the demand is now upon us to create our own rules, our own guidelines. As John Welwood writes in his excellent Journey of the Heart (Intimate Relationship and the Path of Love): "Now for the first time in history, every couple is on their own—to discover how to build a healthy relationship and to forge their own vision of how and why to be together. It is important to appreciate just how new this situation is. We are all pioneers in this unexplored territory."

When I first read that I felt so relieved... a sense of compassion emerged for myself and my friends who have been struggling with relationships. It was as if I no longer had to find some solution (whether ancient or traditionally religious) out there that would somehow make it all right. I was free to be a pioneer—which means making mistakes, hurting people, hurting myself, getting involved in circumstances that were way out of my emotional capabilities, dropping out of the entire scene and then gradually and gently moving back into it.

My point in this all too brief essay is to explore the sacredness of this journey of finding a mate. First off, I cannot overemphasize the need to move slowly... to become genuine friends, to explore and discover honestly who the "other" is (let alone knowing who we are). An intimate relationship is one of the most sacred and precious gifts available to the human species. It gives us an opportunity to open our hearts to another person—to feel the tender openings of love coming our way. Being loved is awesome. It opens old wounds of how we weren't loved as children or how we were abused when certain adults invaded our innocence and natural naiveté. Being loved, feeling the loving energy from the other is like food to a starving man or woman. It is a food from the gods and goddesses given to us to feed our souls.

Many of us freak out when we feel love coming our way let alone knowing how to love others. We're more familiar with romance, titillation, clinging, desperation, complaining, whining and blaming. It's no wonder so many of us have given up on "finding a relationship" since it brings up all the stuff that didn't work in the past: the brutal betrayals, the high expectations, the horrendous sexual fights. What about bringing these truthful dramas and experiences of our unique journey into the new relationship? Not to repeat the past, but to use the past as compost in order to cultivate awareness, curiosity, and the humor that comes with telling our stories... revealing our journeys.

For example, if I find myself babbling on about work or mechanically rubbing my partner's breasts in a certain way that worked before but without feeling what I'm doing—do I have enough balls to stop and say "This doesn't feel right." Or does the woman have enough courage to say, "Where did you go? I can't feel you present with me." And if that occurred, wouldn't it be great to turn the lights on, look honestly into each other's eyes and share what's really going on. To me, that's a turn on! That's what genuine intimacy is all about!

Turning the lights on to all the fantasies, romantic memories and mind games we play with each other in order to get what we think we want. It may appear to be quite scary and very vulnerable to actually initiate a dialogue of truth-telling but often times the truth can act as a very powerful aphrodisiac; more powerful than all those techno-devices they sell in the sex shops and catalogs.

What Does a Man Want?

To be a beloved son, a protective husband,
A provident parent and responsible provider
To be included in a company of men
To accept and endure female empowerment
To be heroic
To live up to his commitments
To be close to a woman who will leave him alone
To please his mother and be loved by his father
To be trusted by those he serves
To do his job without tethers or questions
To be treated fairly
For all to believe he has done his best
To be forgiven for being human
To remain silent, yet understood.

The great question, which I have not been able to answer despite my thirty years of research into the feminine soul, is "What does a woman want? **Sigmund Freud**

The Wake

Douglas "Doc" Moxness, Nurse, Counselor

1969 was a time of worldwide confusion, wars, and torn emotions. JFK's famous speech seemed to make sense. "Ask not what your Country can do for you but, what you can do for your Country." I was 18 and I was ready.

Like most guys in my generation, I'd grown up watching Hollywood Westerns and WWII movies. John Wayne and Audie Murphy showed us how to fight bravely, win the war and get the girl. Actually, I saw myself more as a lover than a fighter but in all the war movies the guys in uniform had it all. The rewards made the risks worthwhile. Since I wasn't going to college it was just a matter of time before Uncle Sam would send me to Vietnam. I hated my stepfather and desperately wanted to get out of his house but failed at every attempt.

My mother, a nurse, had my respect. She was definitely doing her part on the home front. So my best thinking led me to believe that if I enlisted in the Army, I could become a Medic and all my problems would be solved. I would probably work with doctors in a well-protected hospital behind the lines. I would run to the wounded in battle and keep them alive until the choppers got there. At least that's the image I formed by watching the evening news each night around the dinner table. It was a foolproof way to both escape my family and gain their respect. Besides, I was proud to serve my Country like a real man.

So I enlisted in the Army. My entry date was April Fools day, 1969 and the joke was on me. Neither my parents nor my friends reacted as I expected. I thought they'd be happy. No one thought it was the right thing to do. It wasn't lit the movies at all. No one cheered when I marched off to war.

At the Induction Center, standing in line with other guys in our underwear, I still felt confident that I'd made a good decision. A Sergeant was sizing us up and arbitrarily choosing candidates to be sent off to the Marines, Navy or Army. The sense of shock I saw on the faces of those chosen sticks in my mind. I knew I was safe. I hadn't been called. I enlisted. I would be in the Army and having already chosen to be a Medic, I'd probably go directly to some Army Medical School for training.

Boot Camp at Fort Ord was nothing like I imagined. Instead of Anatomy and Surgical Technique, I learned what discipline and regimentation were really about. The Drill Sergeants kept us on forced marches through the sand dunes until we could run all day weighted down with full packs. In spite of being humiliated, intimidated and brainwashed into believing that the enemy was a "commie gook" ripe for the killing, I continued to believe that being a medic was the right choice for me. By the end of training I was in the best shape of my life. Although too young to grow a mustache, I felt every bit as strong and brave as John Wayne.

The next stop was Medic School at Fort Sam Houston in San Antonio, Texas. It was mid summer. Temperatures were pushing 120° and watching films with titles like "How to Apply Wound Dressings" in oven-like Quonset huts put me to sleep. The course was a total blur of boring subjects seen through sweat-filled eyes. It wasn't long before I was wishing I'd remained alert.

At Graduation I received a certificate and my assignment. It was a shock. I felt like those guys I'd seen at the Induction Center being sent off to who knew where. Instead of being stationed in some cushy hospital in Australia or New Zealand, I was ordered to report to Oakland, California for transport to Vietnam and I was there before I realized what happened

I landed in Vietnam under heavy fire in Tan Son Nhut Airport, just outside Saigon. Surrounded by tracer bullets, mortars and rockets, the air-ground crew rushed me off the plane and into a sandbagged bunker. I was scared to death. Two weeks of "In-Country Training" followed. I learned to look for booby traps, all about jungle rot and something called the Black Syphilis. If you got the Black Syphilis they wouldn't be sent home...ever. You'd spend the rest of your days on some remote island awaiting a horrible death. These were no nonsense lessons. I hardly slept for the entire two weeks.

I was assigned to be a corpsman in an infantry division and I found myself in the middle of the war. I was afraid I was going to die and hoped my fear wouldn't show. Would I humiliate myself by pissing in my pants? The men in my squad were waiting to see how I would handle myself under fire. Would I freeze up when they needed me? I didn't have the answer myself. But, when the time came and I heard someone call "Medic," I crawled, head down and shaking like a leaf, to my first casualty. He was hit in the face and I thought I was going to throw up. I remember thinking I wish I had paid more attention to those films back in Texas. Yet, somehow I didn't freeze up or pee. I did what I was trained to do and proved to myself and to the men in my company that I deserved to called "Doc". I felt like a man for the first time in my life.

Combat casualties take various forms. I became totally depressed and believed that each day was my last. I felt guilty and tried to hide it. I was hyper-vigilant, always looking over my shoulder, listening for a noise, a signal, anything that might be out of place. I stopped asking guys for their last names. When not under fire, I drank or smoked pot to mask the pain of being alive. The minute I felt relaxed it would be time to go again. We'd jump into the chopper and fly someplace to fight for the same ground we had taken just a few weeks before. Among my still lingering memories of being a Medic in Vietnam was the task to collect the personal possessions of those who fell or were wounded and taken to a hospital. Putting their things in a box to be shipped out was like but the dreams wouldn't stop. Instead, they became more vivid. I started having nightmares. Some mornings I would find myself drenched with sweat like I'd been running a marathon. I'd wake to find cuts and bruises and not have a clue about what happened during the night. I became terrified of my potential for anger and violence remembering when I had picked up the gun in Vietnam and in a rage started shooting back at the enemy over the bodies of my friends. I heard about other veterans who'd "lost it" and actually ended up hurting innocent people. I was afraid to let myself go. I felt as though it had all been a bad dream. I tried to get on with my life. I was 21 and wanting to go back to school or get a job but I couldn't concentrate on anything for more than a few minutes at a time. Jungle jitters persisted. Hearing a car backfire, I'd hit the ground. I found myself overcorrecting for the least differences. Unable to fit in, I couldn't be with people and I was miserable at home.

Hoping to get away from it all I redoubled my efforts to get my life together and hit the road. For six years, I tried religion and health and became a Buddhist/vegetarian while living as a hermit in the Rocky Mountains. I got married, then separated, and then got back together again more times than I can recall. For no reason, I'd be angry. I quit jobs or got fired. It made no difference. I tried school on the GI bill, but dropped out. I got a divorce. More than once, I considered suicide.

Finally, I turned to the VA for help. Diagnosed with Post Traumatic Stress Disorder, I began attending Veterans' support groups and received individual therapy. The support group brought back even more memories and horrible nightmares but they allowed me to process the war in my mind and put it to rest. Today I'm able to share my feelings about the war and be validated by other veterans.

During the time that most kids grow from adolescence to manhood in the normal way, I was in either in Vietnam or trying to recover from it. When there, the only way I could do what was needed of me was to completely lose myself to duty. If I had thought about me, I wouldn't have been able to run through a line of fire to attend the wounded. I felt like a movie hero because I was doing something that was greater than me while serving a larger purpose. Even though the war I fought has been judged stupid and unnecessary, yet remains in my mind as a surreal nightmare, real people died there. Those real people needed me to be their "doc." From it, I learned to fulfill my personal responsibility no matter what the situation; that even when everything around me seems completely out of hand, I can control my own actions especially when touching the souls of brothers.

When my "tour" ended and I was in one piece, I was sent home. I never received any kind of debriefing or closure from the army. Ignorant of the anti-war frame of mind existing stateside, I arrived at the airport expecting a truly Audie Murphy-type of hero's welcome. Instead I was spit on and called a warmonger and a baby killer by a total stranger with no concern for the sacrifices I had made in his behalf.

While I was away my girlfriend had gotten married and hadn't told me because she heard that soldiers receiving "Dear John" letters sometimes took undue risks and got themselves killed. No one wanted to hear about my problems; not cab drivers, bar tenders, much less old friends. The truth was that it was just too hard to explain my feelings about being in a jungle war where men hunted each other to the death. My mother was grateful to have me home but fearful of hearing my experiences. When I talked about it, she'd start to cry and I'd feel guilty and just clam up. My stepfather wouldn't or couldn't talk about it with me. All he asked was what I planned to do "now" meaning he was anxious to get me out of his house.

It wasn't long before I began denying that I was ever a veteran. I gave away my medals and war memorabilia.

> "The four incentives men must confront are:
> The social reinforcement to men's addiction to female beauty and sex
> Deprivation of the beautiful woman and sex with her until the man guarantees economic security in return
> Status, praise, and other "bribes" in exchange for protecting women, especially if he risks his life or dies doing it, and
> The combination of ritual and religion (e.g., circumcision) that desensitizes men to pain, and music and religion (e.g., "The Battle Hymn of the Republic") to stimulate men to endure pain." **Warren Farrell**, The Myth of Male Power, Berkley Books

Perspective

Ron Thompson, Advertising Executive

I like women. Tough women, sensitive women, beautiful and lovely women; I like them all. Early on I learned that because of my liking them, they liked me too. It meant that they would help me whenever possible. Maybe my liking for them stemmed from never having thought that women were "lesser than" men. And, because they sensed my respect or were taken with my positive attitude, they responded in kind. In any case, our mutual liking has almost always worked in my favor.

I began liking women when I was a kid while observing my three older sisters and coming to understand the competitive sharing and basic male-female personality differences. My interest in their affairs helped me become the object of their affection. Outside on the street or in the schoolyard my liking for female as well as male playmates earned similar benefits. When it came to choosing captains I was selected more than often. Later, in business, my insider's knowledge of women helped me to easily and fairly manage gender politics and protocol. Socially, my female friends allow me preferential treatment noticeably different from the more defensive front used with typically adversarial males. The result is that the majority of my friends are women. I admit their friendships do require more maintenance than for men, but you generally get what you pay for.

It's not like I'm avoiding the rough and tumble manly experience. The idea of a "weaker sex" is far from factual. Women can be as tough as nails. In the stable where I share many hours with female riders and jumpers, they generally exhibit more strength and endurance than most men I've known. I've seen women come down harder on other women than most men would ever dare with either men or women. What impresses me most, and more and more, about women in business today, is their tenacity, their general lack of being intimidated by aggressive forces, and their "break the wall down" approach to tackling problems and pursuing opportunity.

Back in the Sixties when I entered the business world of advertising/marketing/ communications I initially thought that I had to be the front "man" with women in supporting roles. It wasn't that I believed that to be correct. I thought it was something society expected. For many years now, that's hardly been the situation. My industry presented a break-through for women allowing them to design, organize, perform, and make money, in short, to change the rules. Today, the majority of people in the business and marketing and communications professions are women. My link with them remains positive. As I grew in the profession, they spotted me as an ally. The more influential I became in my firm, the more my relationship with female associates, including women who worked for me as well as women I worked for, served to be mutually beneficial. It attracted both clients and revenue. I will never comprehend how anyone, whether male or female, could imagine winning in a war between sexes when there's so much pleasure to be found in peaceful coexistence.

Confession

Craig Nuttycombe, Carpenter, musician

I do not like most men. This is not to say that I don't have male friendships, some going back as far as twenty and thirty years. I treasure them and consider them as blessings in my life. There are also many great men I admire and respect as well.

I do not like most men because their greedy and aggressive behavior has created an unhealthy society for human beings. Most men seem to be motivated by the desire for money and power, a motivation which manifests itself in a culture that is reckless in the use of both human and natural resources, a super competitive culture producing great wealth for the few while the rest of us do the best we can to manage.

Women and minorities especially are victims of such a dominant male perspective as indeed are children who are influenced by violence in films, television, and the evening news. This year our government will allocate 279 billion dollars for 'defense.' A few men will reap profits by creating weaponry destructive to masses of their fellow human beings. The litany of environmental woes created by men is lengthy. The depletion of natural resources, global warming, destruction of rain forests, and pollution of our rivers and oceans are but the tip of an impending disaster. How can men be so uncaring of their own species?

From our earliest training we are taught to not show feelings and to be tough, that money is the road to happiness, and that he who has the most toys in the end is the winner. Fortunately not all men conform to this dominant pattern of male behavior. The men I like best are gentle, caring, compassionate human beings and not driven by the motivation for power and wealth. They find their satisfactions in professions that nurture people.

It is men expressing loving kindness, good will, and a desire to support humanity who are my role models. It is those men who make me proud to be male. The few examples that have positively influenced my life include a downtown LA auto mechanic who impressed me profoundly by being genuinely kind and going out of his way to help others. His behavior became a model for me. Another was a humanities professor who taught me that my true final examination in life would test how I lived as a member of a diverse society.

To Be (a Man) or Not To Be. Is this a Question?

Christof Hillebrand, Wine Exporter (Germany)

My marriage went down the drain. The family company I had inherited from my father was in big financial difficulty from my loss of one of its biggest clients. My girlfriend was unhappy that my divorce was taking too long. The image of success I had built up was gone and I seriously wondered how and where my life had started turning so bad. I felt like a loser. I didn't know what to do or who might help or even how to bring up the subject. My friends talked only of their successes in their jobs, their new cars, sports, their beautiful wives and families. None of them discussed problems unless it was about how they had managed to solve them so well. Thinking that I might be the only loser among them had me on edge and feeling miserable. Knowing, down deep, that men shouldn't give in to feelings made me think that I wasn't even a man. Something had to be done to make things right again.

A bottle of wine per evening, alone in my apartment or with an occasional femme was the obvious medication to try but it merely produced morning after headaches and more feelings of guilt. "Oh God," I asked over and again, "what manner of man am I to be so tied to my feelings, especially feelings of guilt after love-making?" What did feelings have to do with being manly anyway? Did it mean I was a 'softy' and not 'macho'? Many of the women I knew were into what used to be men's jobs and some were even into Martial Arts making the roles of 'provider' and 'protector' open to all. Women were viewing men through newly liberated eyes and it was clear that some women detested macho men while others had no use for weakness. The old definitions of gender limits had changed. TV heroes had it all—strength and sensitivity. Foremost, they were without fear. I was full of it. I thought I might be insane and considered going to a shrink, which would have been but another un-manly move.

A trusted friend offered to help. He lent me a book titled *The Road Less Traveled*. After reading a few pages, I saw it was a shrink-book and shelved it. Alone and at wit's end, I figured the world would be better off without me. Thoughts of ending it all shocked me sufficiently. I took the book from the shelf and read it through. It opened my eyes to an entire new world of emotional-spiritual possibilities. My response to my feelings was both natural and normal. It didn't help me to understand manliness, but I learned that I was at least human. Many men were just like me. I no longer felt alone.

Strengthened, I ventured to attend a "Self-Discovery Weekend for Men" where I met a new group of friends, a doctor, a teacher, a winemaker, and another businessman like me, all asking the same question that had me so bothered. "What does it really mean to be a man?" Through introspection and open discussion of family, educational, and societal patterns, I soon changed my focus to self and the question "Who am I?" The answer: I am free to become what I want to be. I learnt that experiencing and sharing my feelings makes life more complete. I learnt that to understand and combine the masculine and feminine parts of me makes me rich. I learnt to see the commonality of gender without judgment and to respect the difference.

My life has since changed for the better. As a man, considering 'Who I am' instead of 'Who I should be' has enriched my personal and social life and strengthened my self-image. As a man, I can enjoy being playful and expressing my feelings without fear of being less manly for it. Best of all, as a man, I choose what I want to be.

Don't you think that women ask similar questions?

He that hath knowledge spareth his words: *and* a man of understanding is of an excellent spirit.
Even a fool, when he holdeth his peace, is counted wise; *and* he that shutteth his lips is *esteemed* a man of understanding.
Proverbs, Chapter 18, Verses 27 and 28

PART SIX:

FATHERHOOD

Because Father, the classical patriarchal male, dominant protector and provider, is historically claimed to be the parent who "knows best," it's not unusual for both sons and daughters to look first to their father for strength and wisdom.

In this final section, three modern sons, having ascended to the status of father, describe their difficult and precarious situations.

HAPPY-BIRTHDAY-TO-MY-FATHER

Patrick J. Germany (Amal S. Mushad), Photographer

> To my "Father" who led me by the collar;
> Through the ages as I "screamed and hollered".
> Who stood through the winter colds
> And remained "Bold and Steadfast";
> Through all obstacles he forged,
> Stood by me, "Good or Bad".

Never realizing until this day;
What I have is a "Father" indeed.
Wishing you a "HAPPY BIRTHDAY" from me.
The man that was my mother's faithful mate;
Never failed to "Cut the Mustard nor the Cake".

"GOOD-LORD!" Thank you for this fate.
Through your greatness you created;
"HAPPY BIRTHDAY!" to my "Father" on this date,
Thank GOD you made it.

Hiding Out

Barry Williams, Architect, university professor

As I stumbled through the brambles and the waist high summer grasses my brain raced ahead of me thinking of all of the possible places they might be hiding. The last message from the young poet our daughter had befriended warned her that he would not be willing to let her go. I had two distinct missions. The first was to "rescue" my daughter, the second, to knock the prose out of that S.O.B.

The first time I recall literally fighting for something was in my 8th grade drafting class. I had just finished a drawing assignment, a rather complex machine part, and was admiring my work when a class "bully" decided to test my resistance by dumping the graphite from the pencil pointer on my drawing. What I remember best about the incident was the teacher pulling me off of the guy and the class looking on in amazement. Those few minutes changed my life in a couple of ways. Having beat-up the bully added as aspect of 'heroic' to my persona. I could fight when necessary and actually win. Fighting has many veils. I decided on the spot to continue taking drawing classes and after high school I selected architecture as my course of study. I am an architect. I lived and breathed architecture. I designed. I built. I taught architecture. Beyond that I was a father, a dad.

In 1980 my wife and I created cute twin girls. For fourteen years they were good in school, relatively obedient and in general fun to come home to. Being a dad wasn't too hard. I wasn't a 'sidelines' kind of dad. I got involved. I went to their soccer and softball games, attended school plays, and built furnishings for their playhouse, all architecturally correct. But most of all I worked hard at my profession and brought home the bacon. We were the definitive happy family. When our girls entered high school, our lives began to change.

Early in the summer of '94 Marisa let us know that she intended to go with some "friends" to the Rainbow Festival in Shasta. We remembered what those things were like. We didn't skip a beat in saying "No!" It was reminiscent of something that her mother and I might have done in our youth, but certainly not at age 14. We survived, but we were lucky.

Among the many justifications for our response were: 1. Shasta was 400 miles away. 2. The "friends" were poets and artists and homeless (by choice), and 3. Their mode of transportation was the thumb.

Having made our point in a rational manner, the case was closed. The next afternoon Marisa was gone. She left a note saying that she was on her way to the Rainbow Festival and would be home in a week.

The angry afternoon turned to anxious evening, then to terrible night, a truly lousy night. My wife was in tears, "How could she do this to me?" My domain as father-protector was compromised and I wanted to kick the shit out of someone. We didn't sleep well. The next morning we phoned everyone including the police where we filed a Missing Person Report. Police focused on one part of the description: Color of hair. Answer: Blue. According to the psychologists in blue, we should have suspected rebellion when our daughter died her hair. Not much help. We called the police in Shasta. "Blue hair? Most of the kids at the festival will have colored hair. That's why they call it the Rainbow Festival, sir." I planned to leave for Shasta in the morning.

Before leaving, we received a call from the mother of one of Marisa's companions. She in turn had just gotten a call from her son and learned that they had missed their ride and were still in town. She had no idea as to where they'd spent the night but said that she could hear construction noises in the background.

We live in a model city with temperate climate, natural beauty, and low crime, comfortable by many standards. Homeless transients find ready shelter and generous charity here. As a local architect on committees studying the problem, I had learned of several areas where the homeless stayed when opting not to stay in a shelter. One such place was just a few blocks from our house, near the railroad tracks I suddenly remembered that they were doing construction there. I had figured it out. I was there in a flash.

Hoping to catch a glimpse of Marisa, I sized up the situation from a distance. The place was fully occupied. Various types and sizes of camps were randomly spaced all along the creek bank. My head was spinning. My life as an architect was on hold. Who would take my appointments and maintain the continuity I'd established? The bigger issue was getting through the gauntlet unscathed with daughter in tow. How would I be perceived…as angry 'truant officer' parent or as loving father? Then, it suddenly came to me. I can't tell you what it was exactly, but something made me see that I was involved in perhaps the most serious situation I had ever faced in my life and that this might be the most important day in all of our lives. Although I was angry with her, the only thing that mattered at that moment was getting her back safely. At that instant I realized what it meant to be a father and care for a child no matter what had transpired or no matter how many problems they'd created.

It was a warm late summer morning. Some water still rippled in the creek. In many ways it was a beautiful setting. I thought "I should come here more often." Following the trail from camp to camp, I talked with someone at every stop. Some were awake, already brewing coffee, others, half asleep, were barely coherent, and others refused to be stirred. They were a mixed group, predominantly males, of different ages and races. Some were open, friendly and eager to help, some untrusting and evasive…just like ordinary people living in comfortable houses in our neighborhood. No one had seen Marisa. I hadn't found her. Returning home alone was not part of my plan.

At home my wife had just gotten another call from the poet's mother. "He'll be leaving soon, hitching a ride to Shasta." This time she detected the distinct sound of high-speed traffic in the background. I remembered maps of homeless camps along the creeks, in particular one that bordered the freeway.

Minutes later I was following a path along the bank of another creek, my adrenalin pumping harder than ever. Moving too quickly, I fell and rolled down the bank through thorny brush. I hurt like hell but it didn't matter. I could only imagine saving Marisa. The camps were vacant; hunter-gatherer occupants already out for the day. Only one camp belonging to an older couple, perhaps in their Sixties, showed life. It looked as though they'd lived there for years. Everything was compartmentalized, the eating area, sleeping area, etc.: a better job than most of my students were producing in Design Class. I asked them if they had seen a girl with blue hair, "my daughter." They looked at each other and then shook their heads. I thanked them and ran on. Struggling through the creek, abandoning any thought of staying dry, I heard someone yelling at me. It was the old man. I turned and headed back to his camp. Had I said "a girl with blue hair"? I nodded. He apologized, saying he thought I had said a girl with a blue shirt. Yes, the blue-haired girl and some others were at their place last night talking about a music festival they were heading for. He had told them about a place where they could bed down and not be bothered. "Cross the creek and up the bank on the other side. Make a left turn at Willie's, the one with all of the bicycles. Then go straight ahead to the trees. They should be there."

Though somewhat loose, I followed his directions easily. Nearing the trees my heart was pounding. I saw two sleeping bags. I didn't know what to expect. Would they be there? Would there be a big confrontation? Long dark hair was sticking out of the top of one of the bags. Then, barely visible inside the top of the second bag was a lock of blue hair. I had never liked her hair that color, but at this particular moment I loved it. It was beautiful. I gently nudged her. She turned and looked at me with very sleepy eyes as she'd done myriad times before. I said, "It's time to come home." She asked, "How did you find me?" and I wearily replied, "It's my job." I still don't know how to put into words all that I had discovered that day, but whatever else had importance in my life, above all I was Dad.

Papa

Milton Mannix, Poet

Thumbs swung from his suspenders;
He condemned while on rocking heel.
Tombstone patriarch, he waited; watched me grow
And not a syllable speared to pop our stoic seal.
His dumb message emerged from inside a deeper recess-
A trifle more ominous to confront but easier to feel.
Yet, I managed to ignore it, to its bold face…
Why? calloused paws failed to swipe the threatened blow…
In defiance of nature's time honored pace,
I struck out, off-beat; doing whatever 'I felt I should!'
Begot myself into and through sundry riots;
But, Be Damned if he weren't right, and I turned out no good.

Fathers

Bill Kiely, School teacher, events promoter

Children often miss the best of what their parents have to give.
When first we encounter our elders we are too much in need. We
grasp, we suck and tug at these people. By the time we are ready to
meet them they are gone.

My father was not a great fan of wee ones. The details of children overwhelmed him. The father-heat he offered came second
hand, as if from the next room. It was the idea of a child that
appealed to him. The possibilities, the new map not yet rolled
flat. Much of the time he was with us he seemed to be readying us
for his absence. Insurance policies, college funds, the short term
meeting with the long range thought behind his brow. He found
his strength away from us, yet he faithfully returned home with
gleanings for our upturned beaks. To hunt, return, hunt again.

The raptor in my father was full-fledged, the nest chilly but well stocked.

When he took his leave I was a young man of thirty-two, he a tired man approaching sixty-five. He died by his own hand, but he did so without histrionics. He left as if for an appointment, can't reschedule, your mail's on the table. His affairs had been well arranged, his hopes and his regards well detailed and notarized. Being here had been a struggle, but his sudden exit was made to appear unremarkable. Take a note. I'll get back to you. It was maddening, but then he always was stiff with goodbyes.

He had been a healer, a bow-tied physician in an age of house calls. I formed the early impression that all fathers carried handsome black bags through the front door following a day's work. After his leaving, I learned how much I had warmed to that medical bag. All the ointments and swabs, the syringes and small flashlights seemed to command well-being. Even so, it wasn't the hardware that kept disease at bay, it was the man's withering glance, the doctor's well-focused anger. A virus, a tumor had little hope for fair play near this man. He looked over his reading glasses to meet an illness straight on, nose-hair to nose-hair. He would scour his hands, clear his throat, and engage the beast. He would of course lose the war, but I was in awe of the jaw-clenched battles.

We are, many of us, marked by a decade that was our own. My father bore the imprint of the mid-sixties, a time when this country took issue with itself. This was the moment of the runaway, the long-haired short-tempered refugee from America's heartland. The pathology of rebellion was my father's chosen game. He relocated to San Francisco and forsook the syringe for the interview. He listened still to heartbeats, but slyly now, from across the room. His previous patients had surrendered to infirmity; his new ones surrendered to no one. Their mind's eye bloodshot from LSD, the recently admitted cried out for a new sort of cure.

My father, sanity's true believer, took over as the policeman made a quiet exit. His doctor's bag now redundant, my father spent his days among the mind-blown. Dad's private life, never a picnic, seemed all the more manageable next to this firestorm among the young. His patients spent their days on the ward listening to The Doors, over and over. He spent his nights listening to Chopin, interrupted now and then by a siren, a curb-side shout. It was for him a kind of peace.

It is likely that my father's deepest affections were offered up to these strangers, the truly needy. By the time he arrived home he was empty, going through the motions. There seemed to be an unspoken pact between us and Dad: we would agree never to manifest anxiety, he in turn would promise never to play The Doc. And of course we broke the pact repeatedly, my father perhaps the worst offender. Small lies, and the pain they enshroud, entered our household against his strict command. Powerless to embrace us, he felt compelled to ferret out our half-truths. He would sense a fib and flashlight it. Some remote form of love, all this, but it left one unwarmed. He was a troubled man giving it his best.

When he died we sons and daughters rushed together to meet his absence. Reading his note, we shuddered and comforted in turns. I remember telling my sister that I felt robbed, that I needed one or two more days just to talk with him. "What would you say?" she wanted to know. I've no idea. Perhaps I am saying it here, perhaps one can never give words to it. We do tell each other less than we mean to; we harbor far more than we are able to share. This silence becomes its own message. We monitor it closely, straining our necks to get it all.

Self-Inflicted

Don Koberg

Through the shaving glass
A steamy casket lid
I see my father's face
His spermatose reflection
Me
We smirk and pose
What silliness we are, the both of us
The one.

It was just last week
Back six score and more
Tyro macho mustached he
Prodding whining toddler
Me
To be a man
The tutor and the taught
So much to learn with little to choose
So little time and none to lose
All for naught
As he dissolves I too
Am on my way
Naturally.

After Shave

Stacey Warde, Activist

I was three when I made my first memorable encounter with anger and fear. My father, 23, had just put his fist through the wall next to the mirror in our bathroom, where he had been shaving. He was big and strong, a muscular construction worker, and I had been admiring his potential as my protector until his arm, like the bolt action of a high-powered rifle, cocked itself tightly beside his washboard stomach and sprung suddenly and smoothly into the wall before him.

I slipped quietly away, stifling my natural curiosity, not asking him what was wrong. Was he going to hurt my mom? Would I be next? Should I be scared?

My father's anger stands as a clear milestone in my development as a male child: if a man can't find something (in this case, 'Old Spice' cologne) or, if he can't have his own way, then he can lose his temper, lash out and destroy something, or someone. Worse yet, I learned that when a father abandons his family (as mine did one year later, and as my mother's father did when she was four) he doesn't need to worry about who might have been hurt in the process.

I guess my father was under a lot of pressure, trying to support a young wife who bore his first child at 17 and his second child at 19. I'll never know what caused him to vent whatever it was in such a violent way. Maybe his boss at the construction site jumped on his case about not getting to work on time. Maybe the threat of communism, daily pushing its way into the American psyche in 1961, was on his mind. Or maybe he just had a lousy day of surfing, trying to escape it all at the beach.

My father died of a brain tumor at 45. Just when I began thinking of tracking him down to ask him where the hell he'd been for the last 20 years, he died. He left this world much the same way he left his family (without warning or fanfare). He simply left, which seemed fine with my mother. Relating the news of his death, she may as well have been commenting on the weather.

"Oh, by the way," my mother said, as I cut several slices out of an apple for a mid-morning snack, "Jim died."

"Who?," I asked, dropping my knife and feeling stunned, like a defeated boxer not knowing what hit him.

"Jim," she repeated, "your father."

I can imagine my father trying to unravel the mix of guilt and anger in his head (the way men do when they furrow their brows trying not to feel anything) until it began to explode, giving birth to an alien growth that would put him out of his misery less than two weeks after his first blackout.

What he was thinking at the end, I'll never know? Did he think about me? Surely, if I could talk to him now I'd tell him what a bastard he was for leaving me. I might cock my fist back and let it fly into the wall. Then, maybe, I'd hug him and tell him I understand how he must have felt. But do I?

As I approach 40, I've been wondering how much I have in common with this man, of whom my most powerful recollection is his anger. I'm careful to note any growths on my head and watch for signs of blacking out. I've done my best to be a better father to my 9-year-old daughter, who has lived with her single mom since she was a baby.

I could argue that I haven't abandoned her, even though we have not lived under the same roof for more than eight years. At least we visit one another. At least she knows who I am, and that I'm available.

My rationalizing sounds trite. I feel guilty and angry (guilty for not being a better father, angry for having been abandoned by mine). I understand a man's desire to throw a temper tantrum. It feels quite natural at times. But I hope men in the millennia to come will not forget their children, nor let their anger, frustration and fear drive them away from themselves and their families.

0-595-22780-5